T0069394

Cover photo: © ZUMA Press, Inc. / Alamy Stock Photo

ISBN 978-1-4950-5882-0

HAL•LEONARD®
CORPORATION
7777 W. BLUEMOUND RD. P.O. BOX 13819 MILWAUKEE, WI 53213

Visit Hal Leonard Online at
www.halleonard.com

All I Ask

Registration 8
Rhythm: Ballad

Words and Music by Adele Adkins,
Philip Lawrence, Bruno Mars and Chris Brown

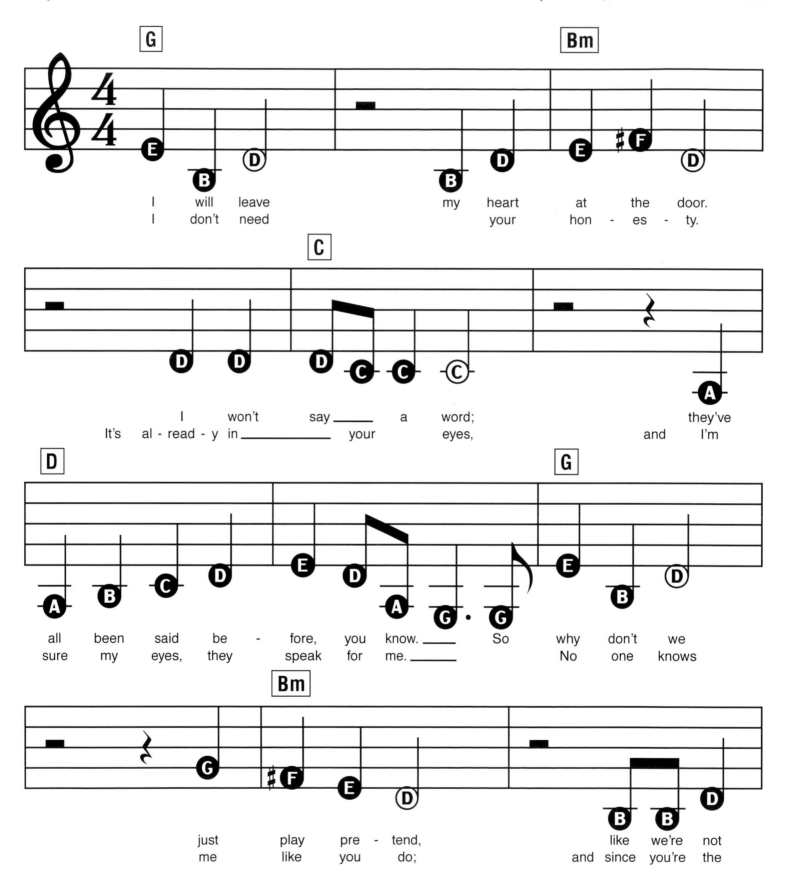

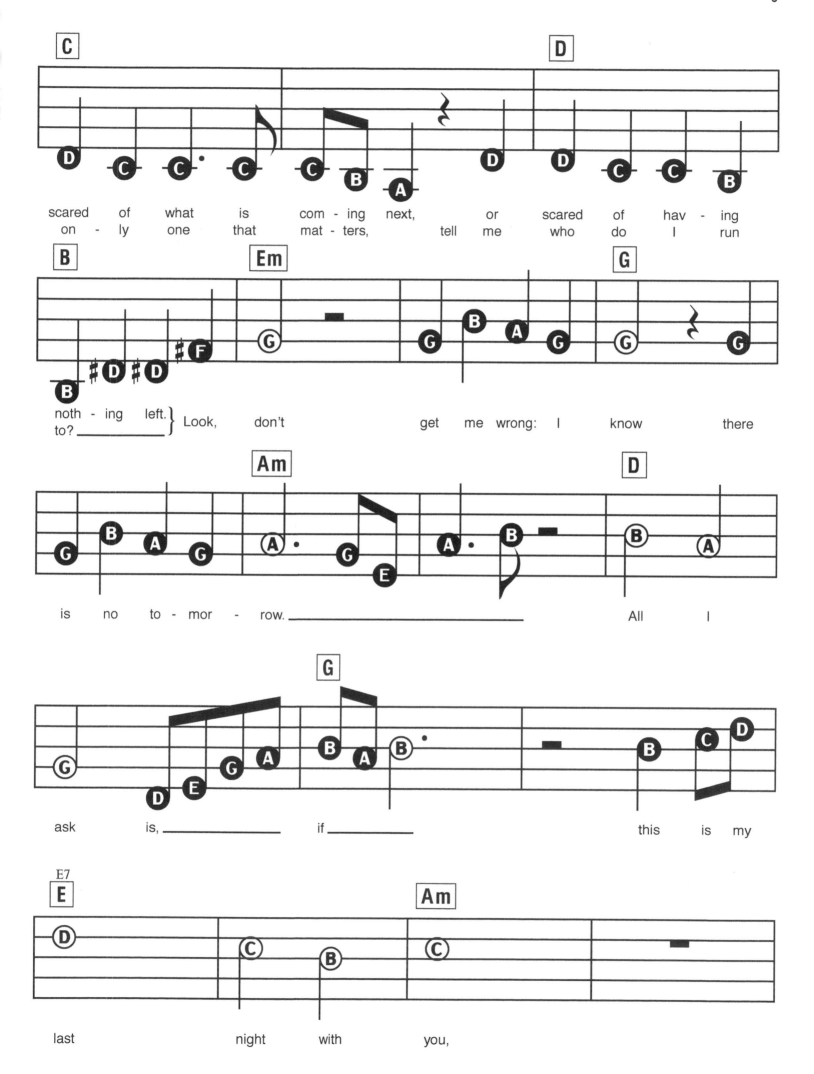

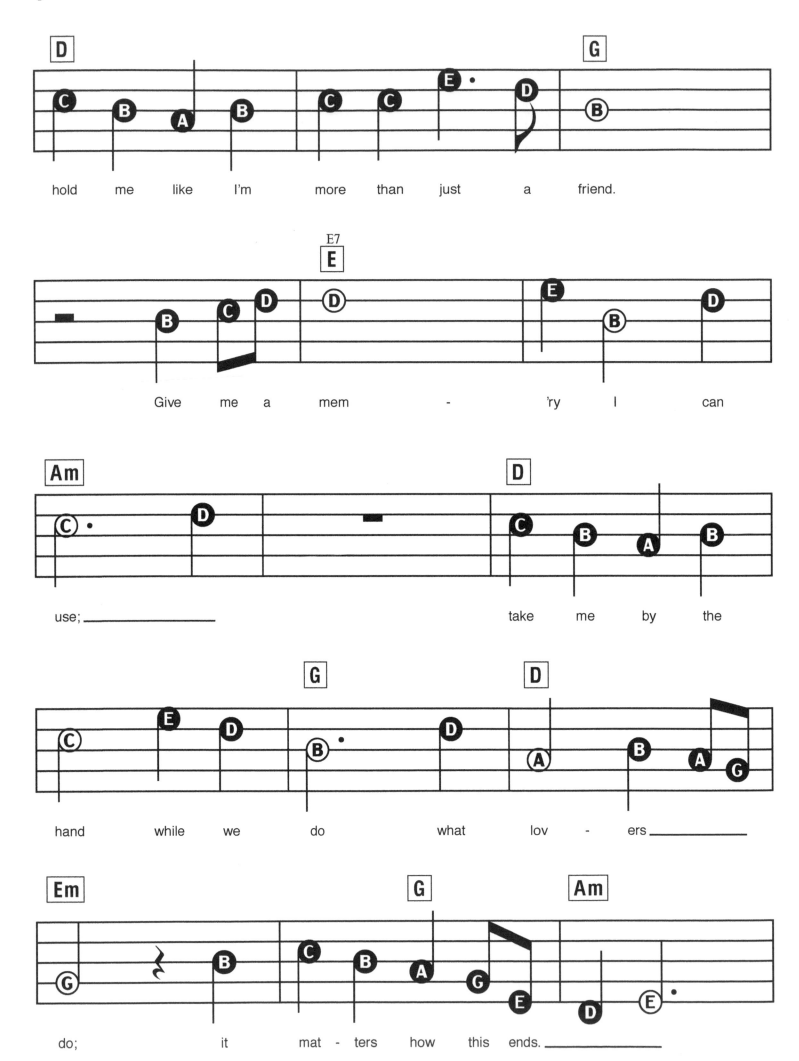

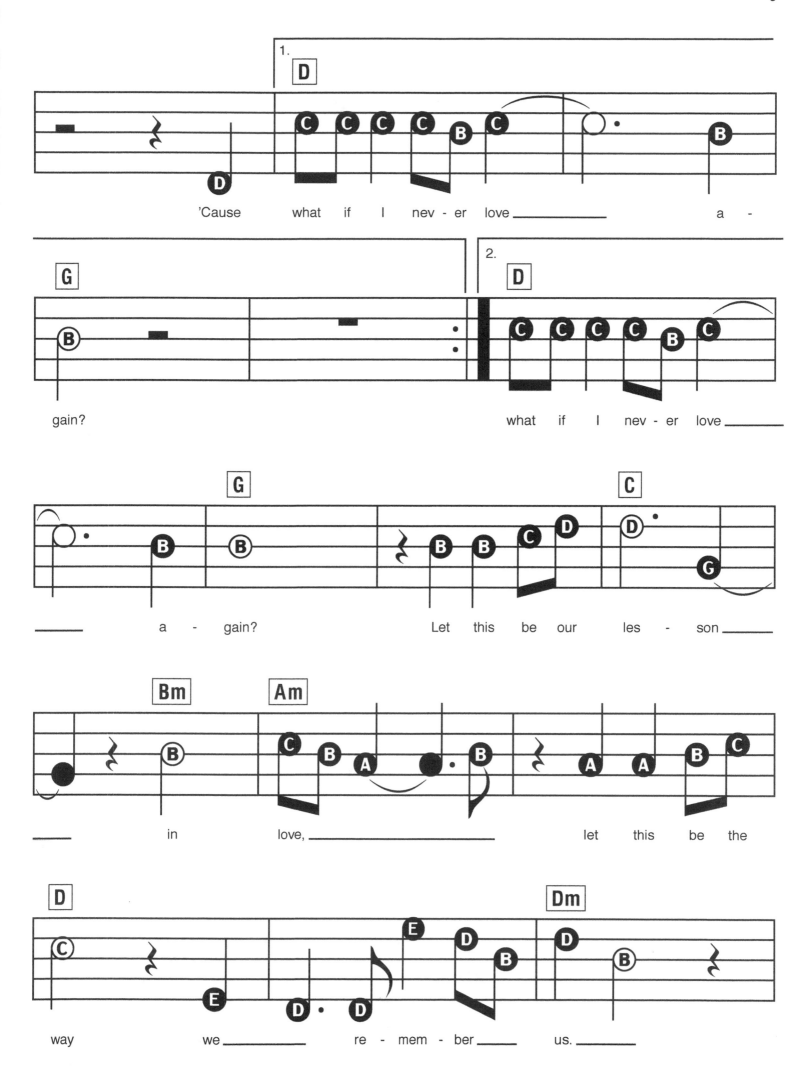

6

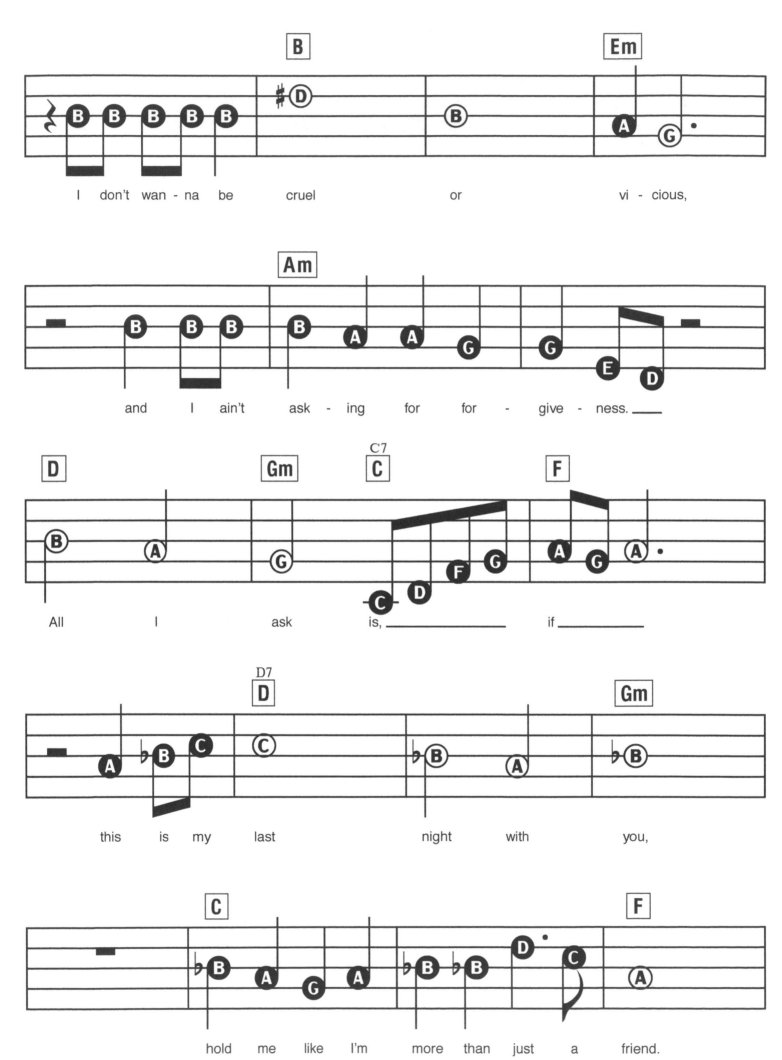

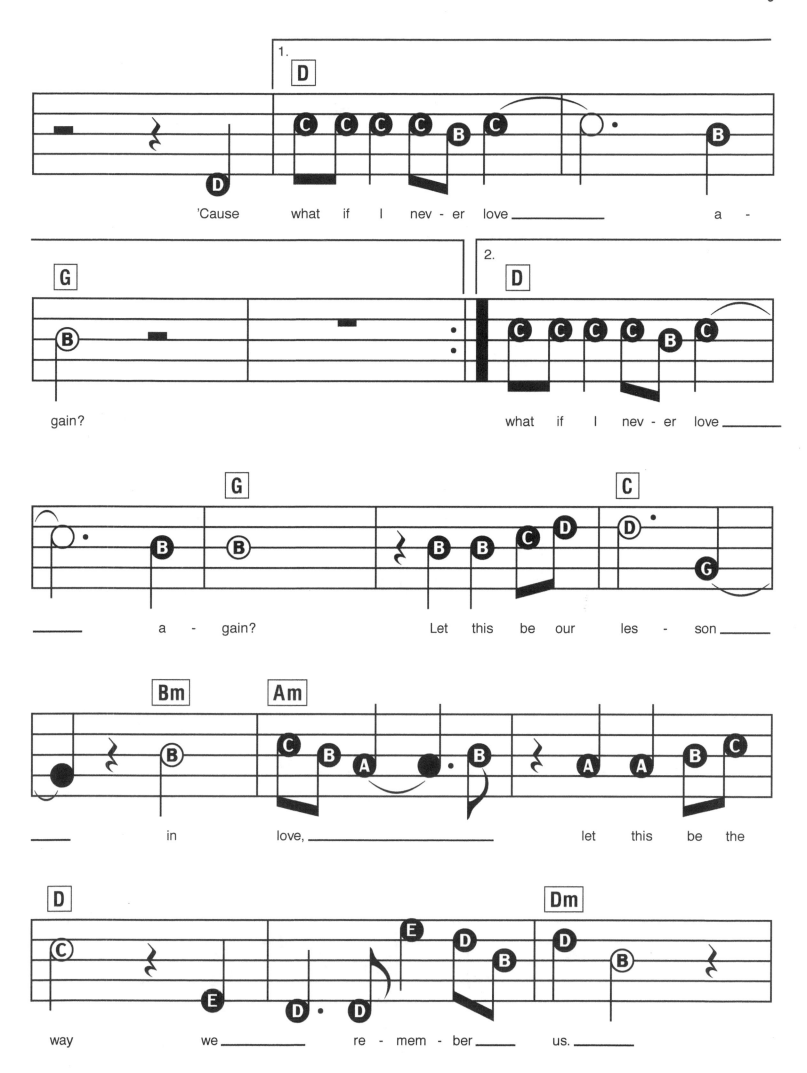

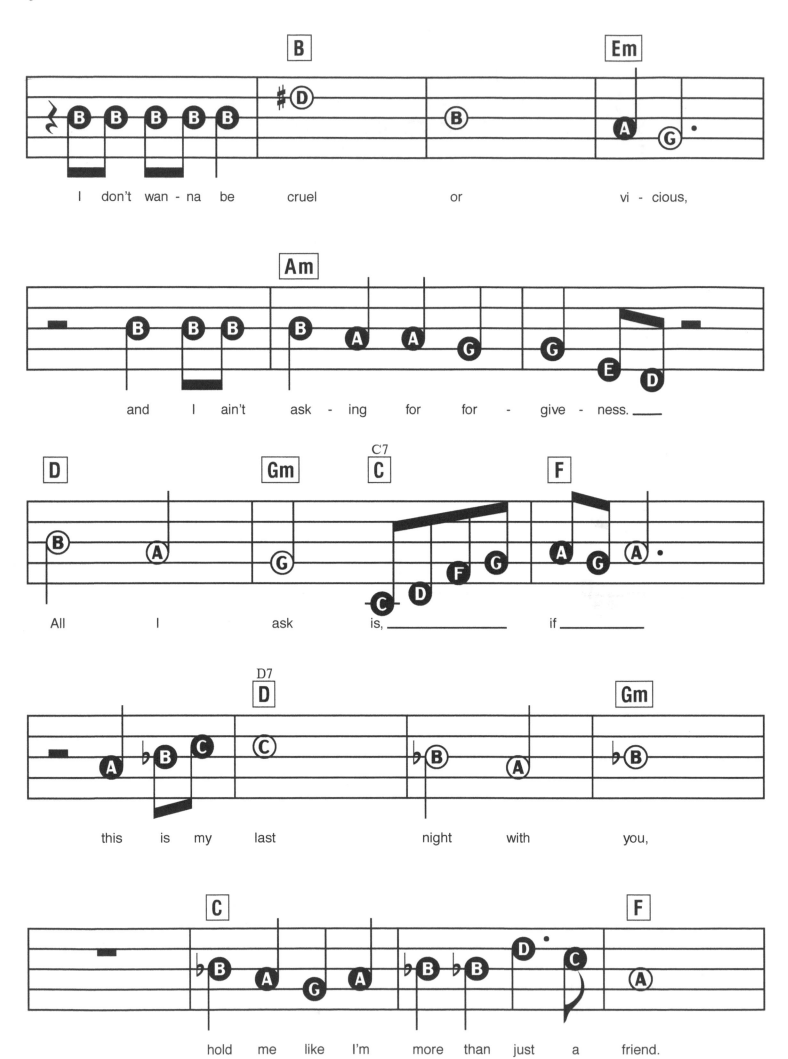

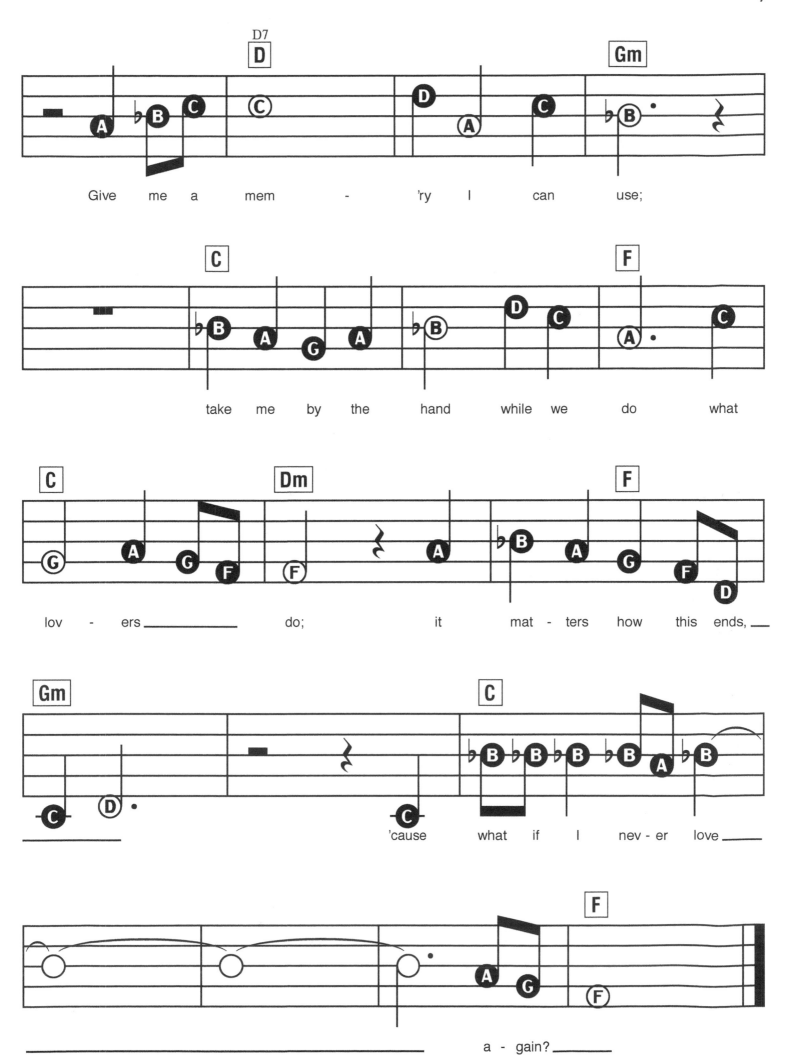

Chasing Pavements

Registration 1
Rhythm: 8-Beat or Rock

Words and Music by Adele Adkins
and Francis Eg White

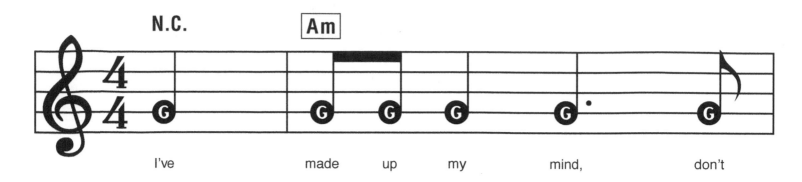

I've made up my mind, don't

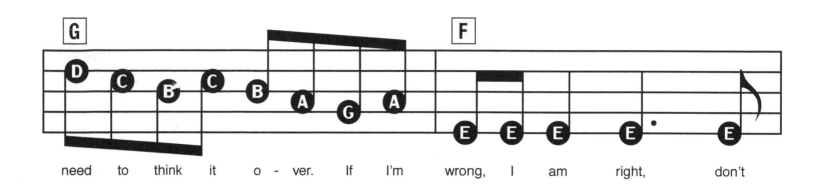

need to think it o - ver. If I'm wrong, I am right, don't

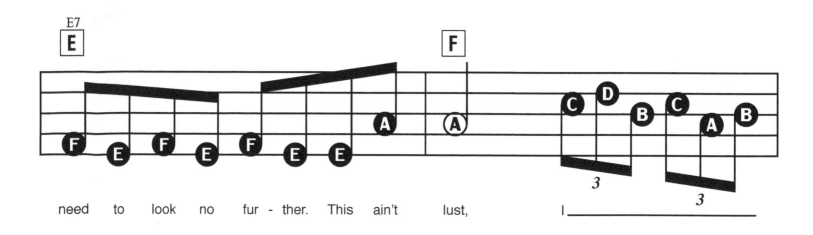

need to look no fur - ther. This ain't lust, I

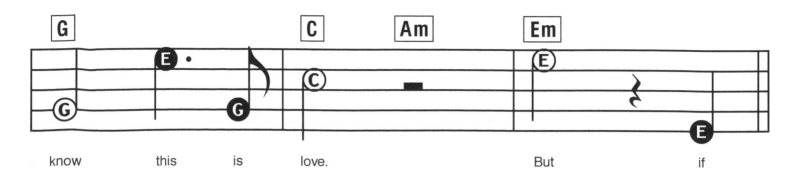

know this is love. But if

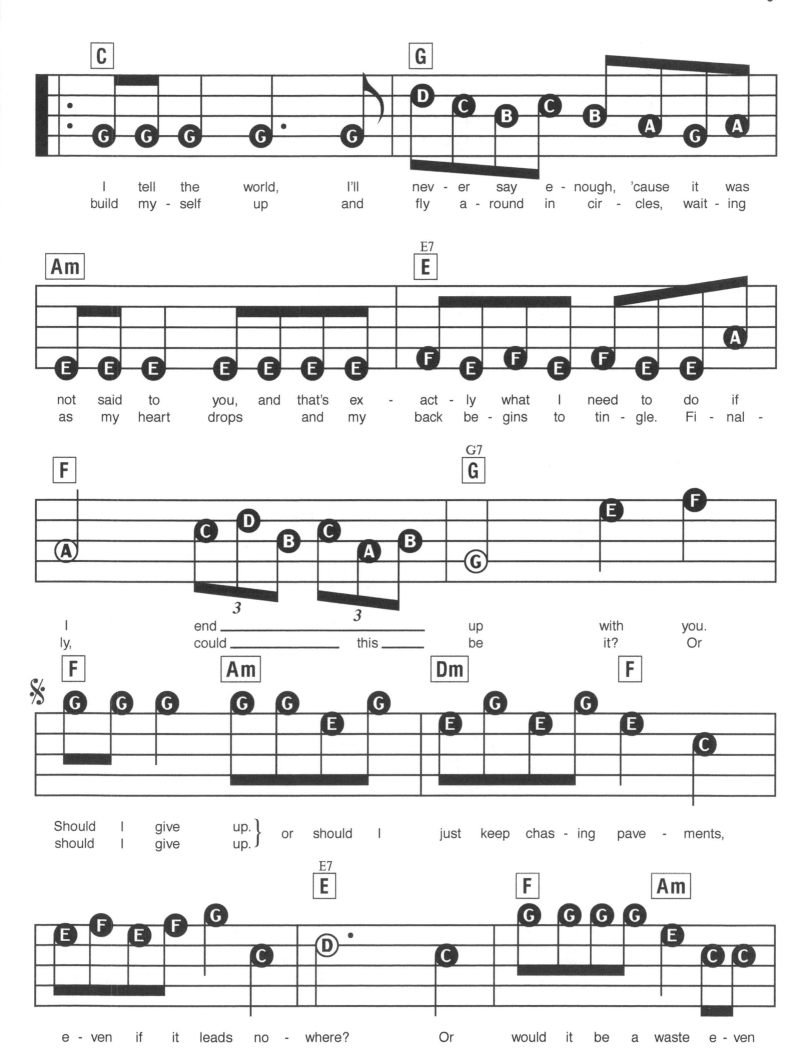

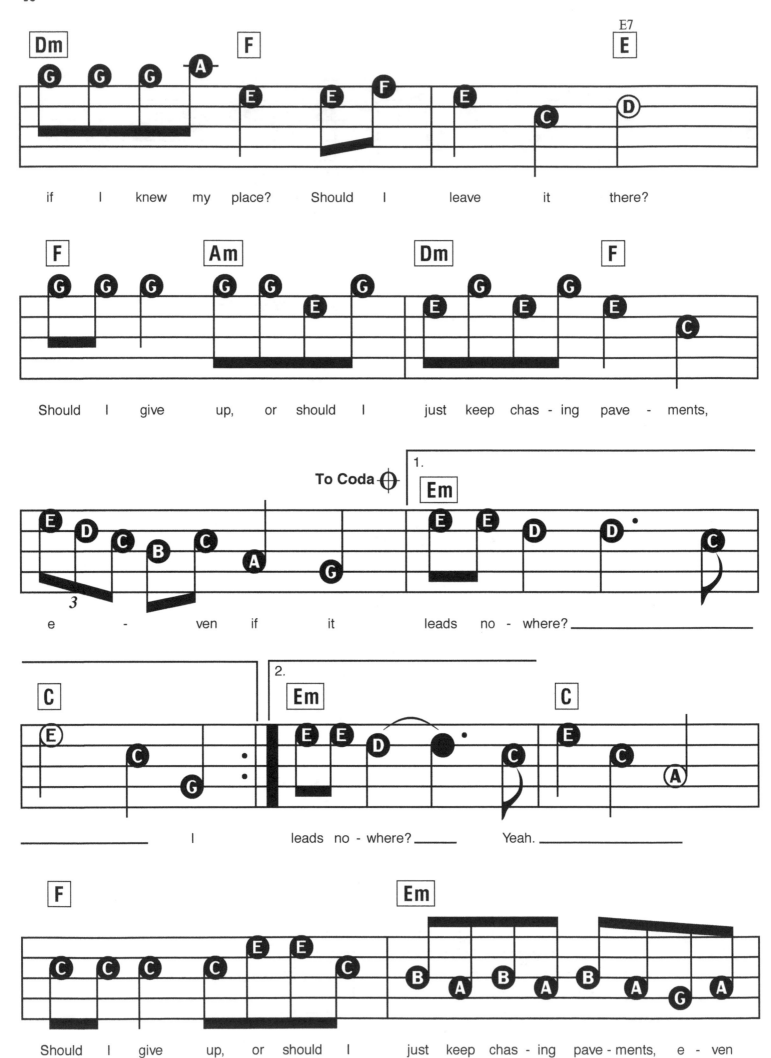

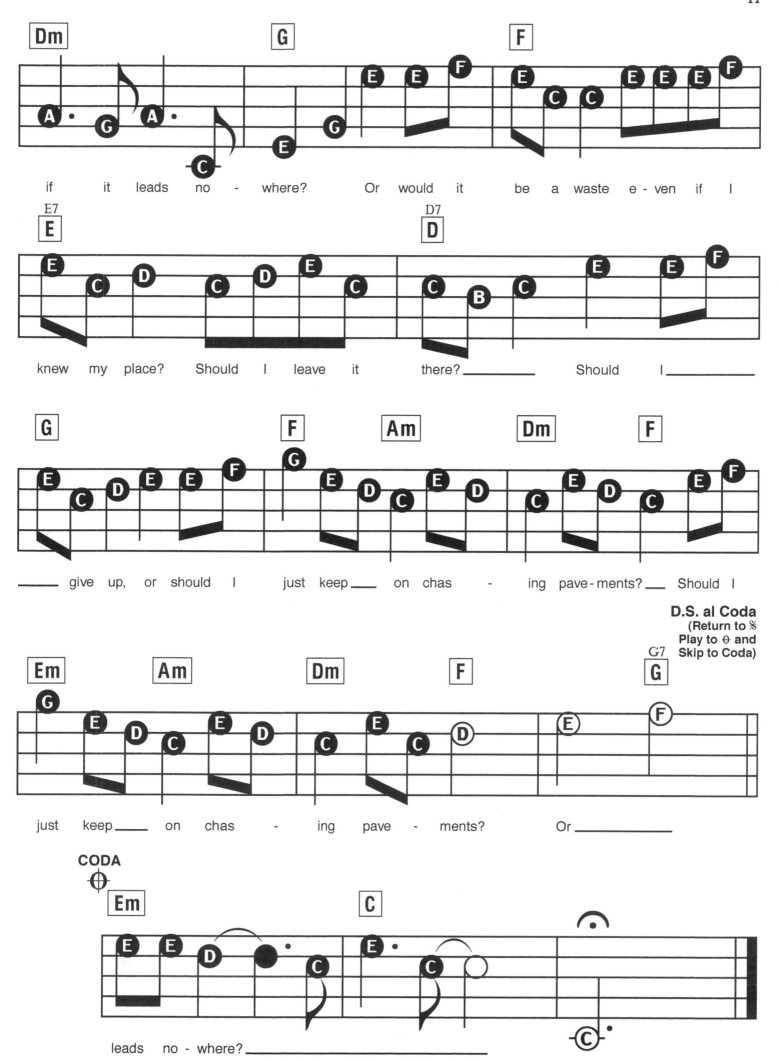

Hello

Registration 8
Rhythm: Ballad

Words and Music by Adele Adkins
and Greg Kurstin

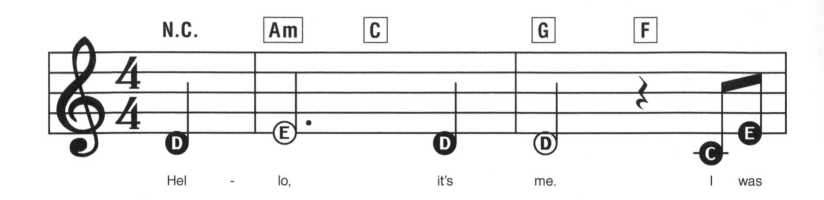

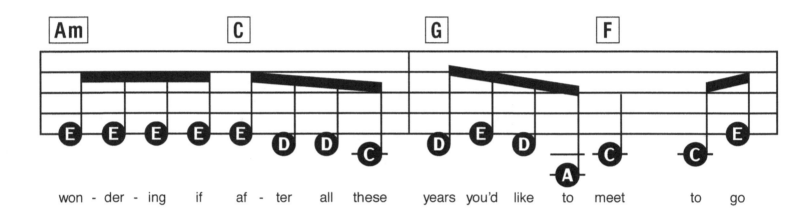

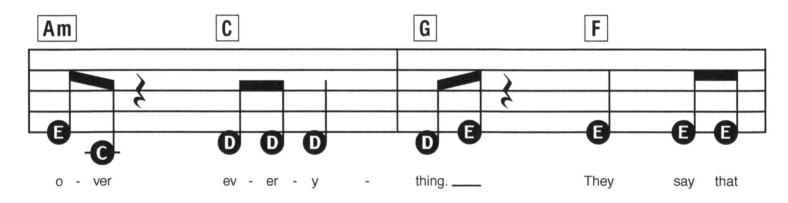

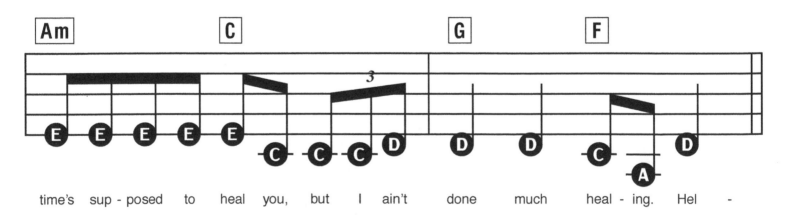

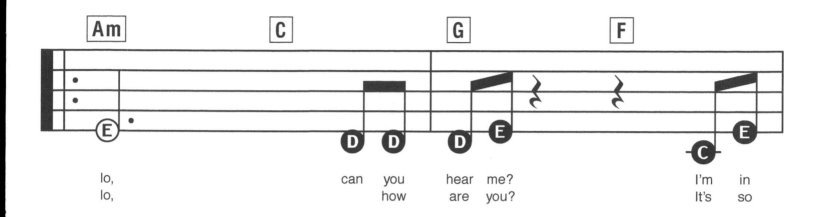

| Am | C | G | F |

lo,   can you   hear me?   I'm in
lo,   how are you?   It's so

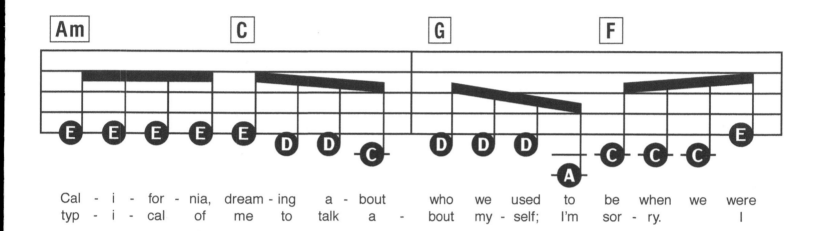

| Am | C | G | F |

Cal - i - for - nia, dream - ing a - bout who we used to be when we were
typ - i - cal of me to talk a - bout my - self; I'm sor - ry. I

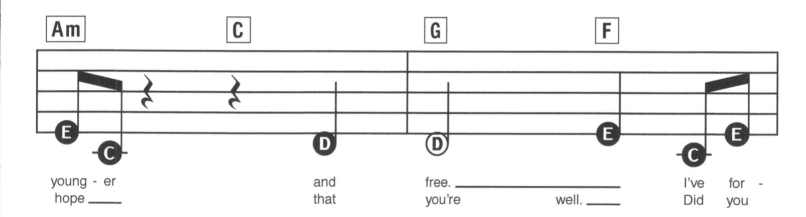

| Am | C | G | F |

young - er   and   free. _____   I've for -
hope ____   that   you're   well. ____   Did you

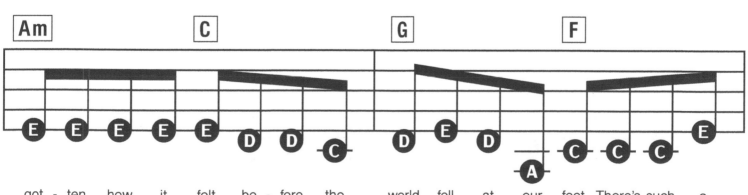

| Am | C | G | F |

got - ten how it felt be - fore the world fell at our feet. There's such a
ev - er make it out of that town where noth - ing ev - er hap - pened? It's no

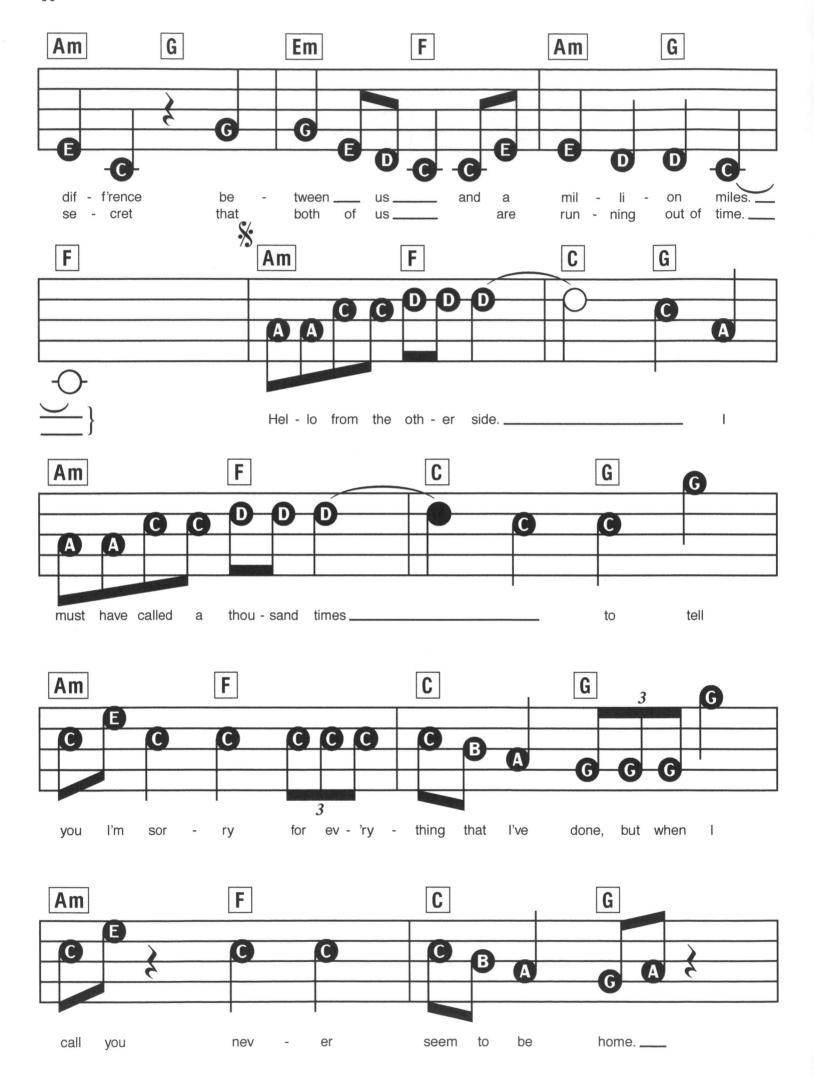

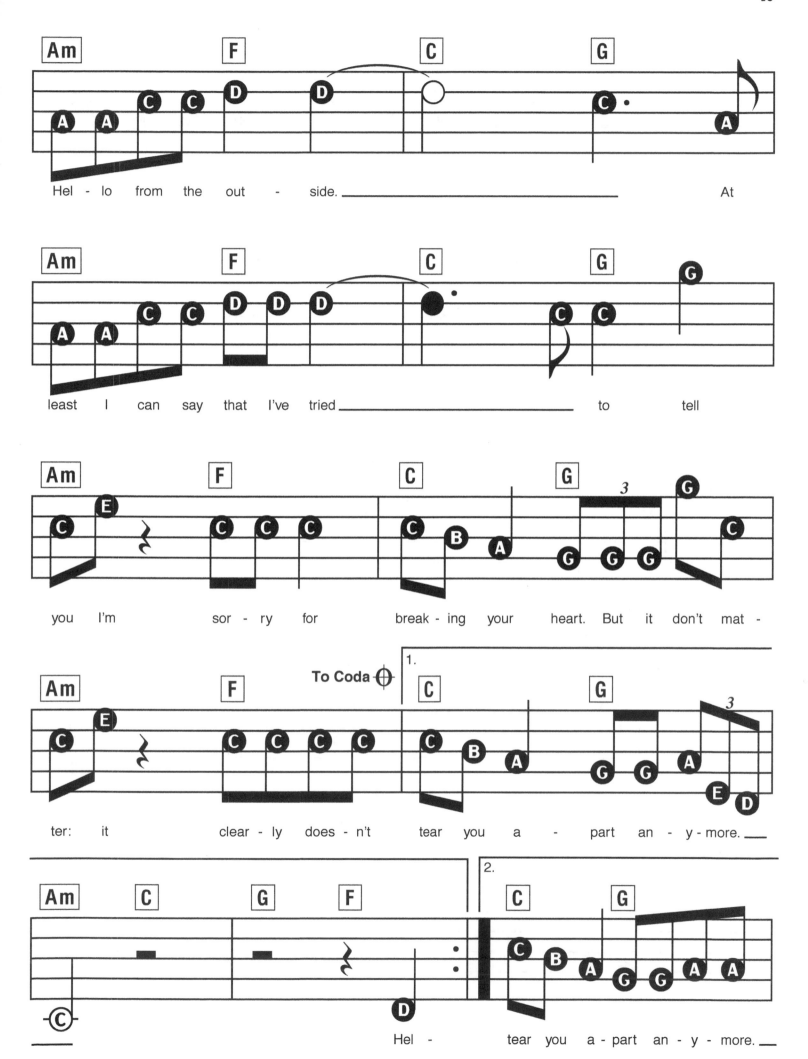

16

(Instrumental)

D.S. al Coda
(Return to %
Play to ⊕ and
Skip to Coda)

CODA

tear you a - part an - y - more. _____

(Instrumental)

Make You Feel My Love

Registration 8
Rhythm: Ballad

Words and Music by
Bob Dylan

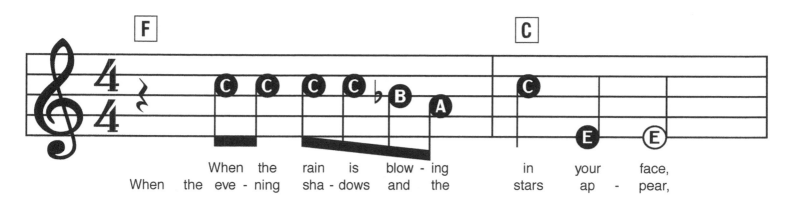

When the rain is blow-ing in your face,
When the eve-ning sha-dows and the stars ap - pear,

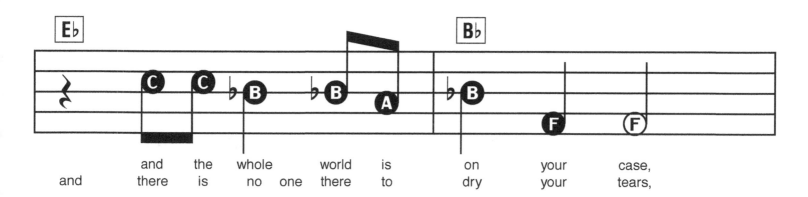

and the whole world is on your case,
and there is no one there to dry your tears,

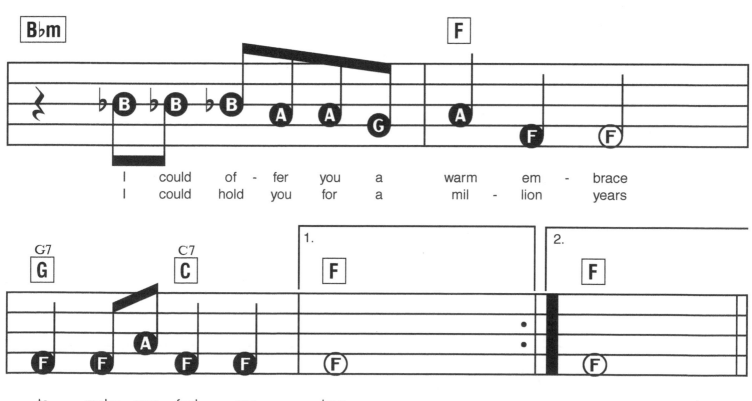

I could of - fer you a warm em - brace
I could hold you for a mil - lion years

to make you feel my love.
to make you feel my love.

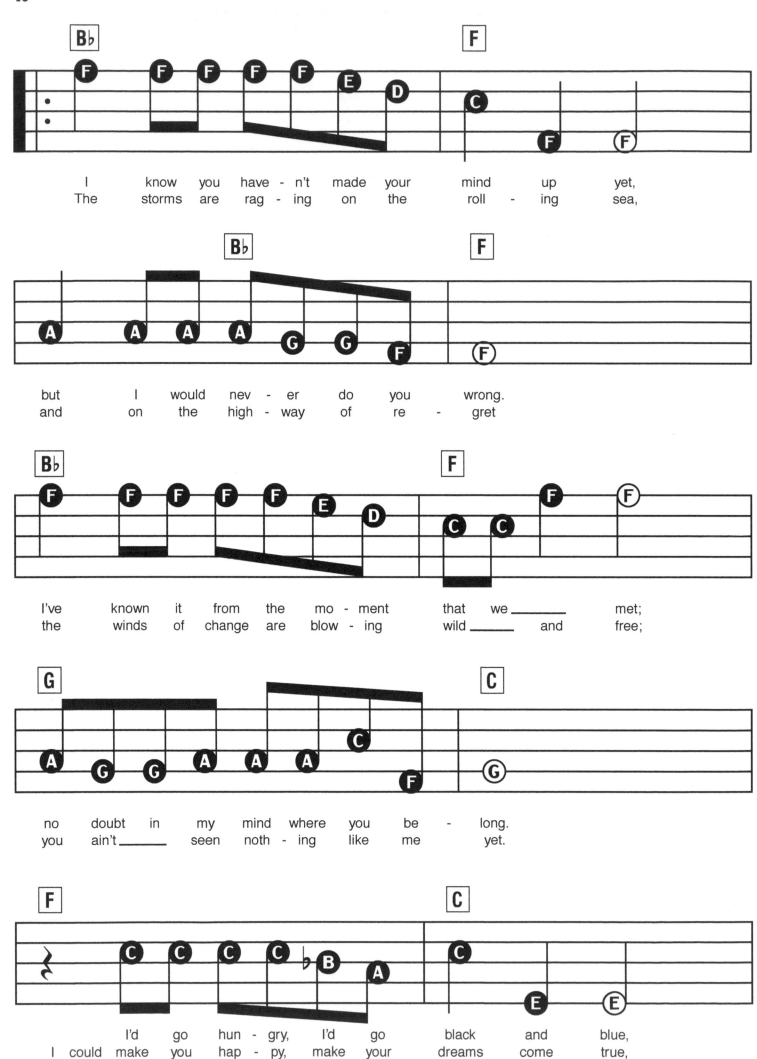

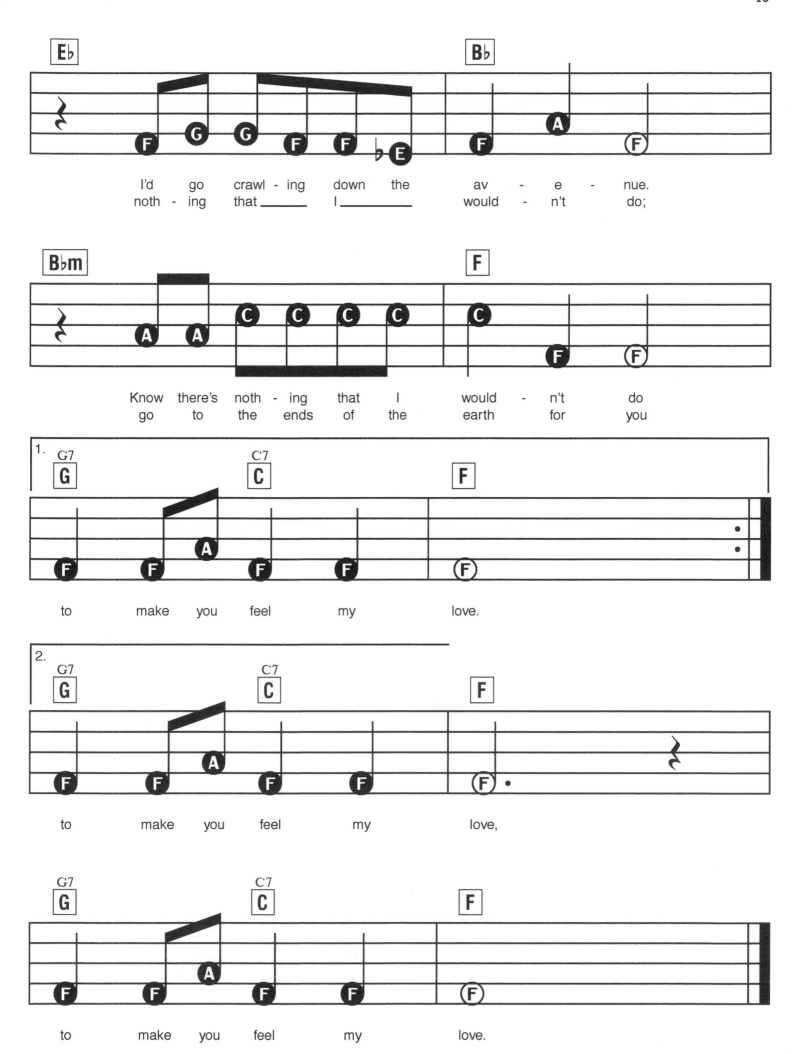

Hometown Glory

Registration 8
Rhythm: Ballad

Words and Music by
Adele Adkins

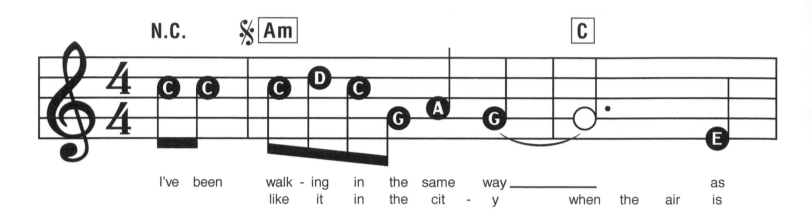

I've been walk-ing in the same way _____ as
like it in the cit - y when the air is

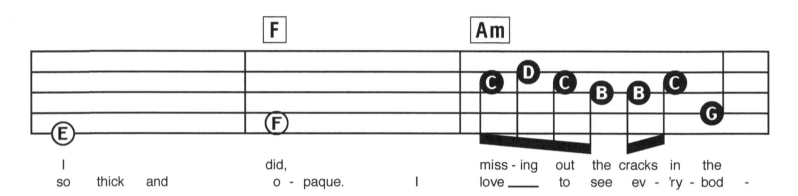

I so thick and did, o - paque. I miss-ing out the cracks in the
love ____ to see ev - 'ry - bod -

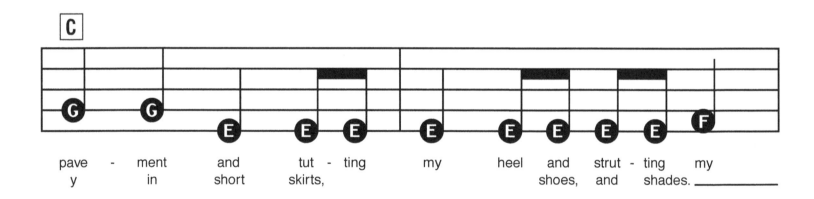

pave - ment and tut - ting my heel and strut - ting my
y in short skirts, shoes, and shades. _____

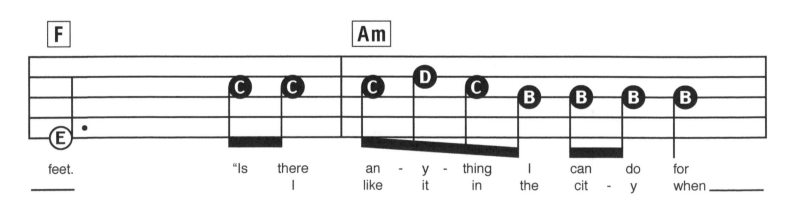

feet. "Is there an - y - thing I can do for
I like it in the cit - y when _____

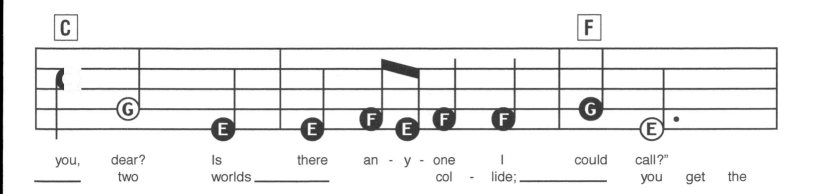

you, dear? Is there an - y - one I could call?"
_____ two worlds _____ col - lide; _____ you get the

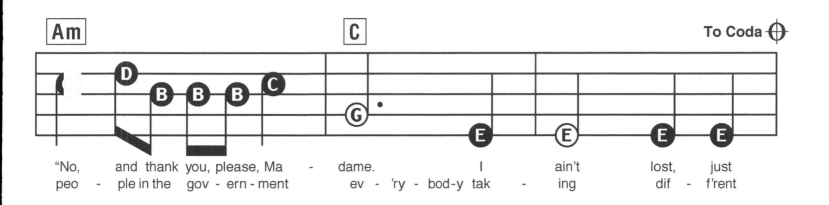

"No, and thank you, please, Ma - dame. I ain't lost, just
peo - ple in the gov - ern - ment ev - 'ry - bod-y tak - ing dif - f'rent

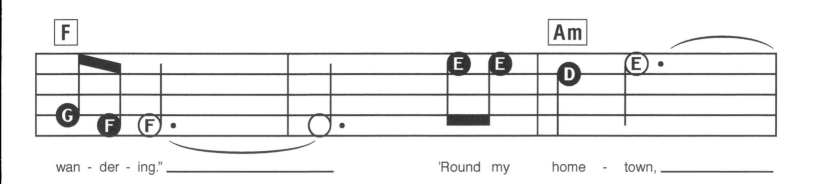

wan - der - ing." _____ 'Round my home - town, _____

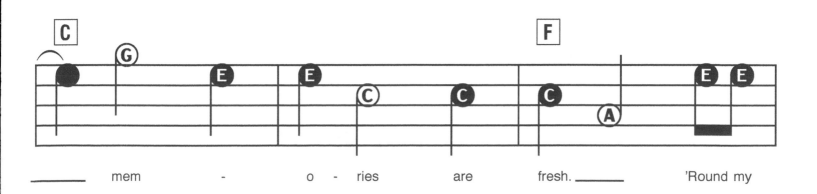

_____ mem - o - ries are fresh. _____ 'Round my

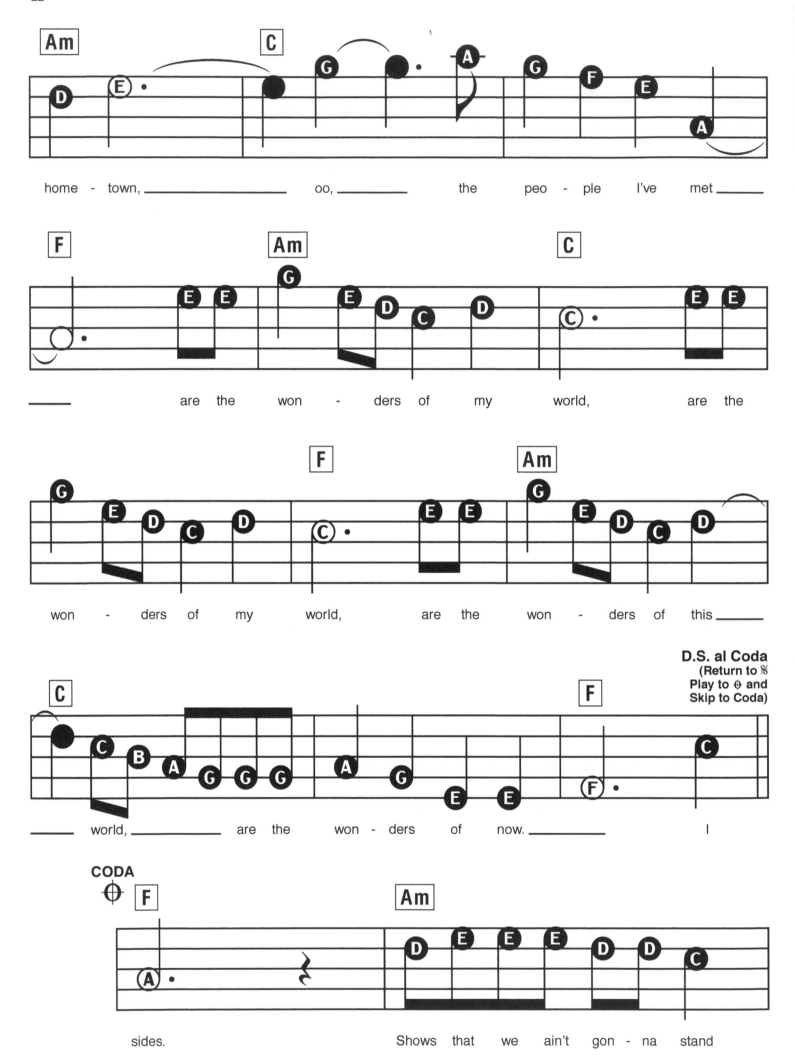

home - town, _____ oo, _____ the peo - ple I've met _____

_____ are the won - ders of my world, are the

won - ders of my world, are the won - ders of this _____

D.S. al Coda
(Return to %
Play to ⊕ and
Skip to Coda)

_____ world, _____ are the won - ders of now. _____ I

CODA

sides. Shows that we ain't gon - na stand

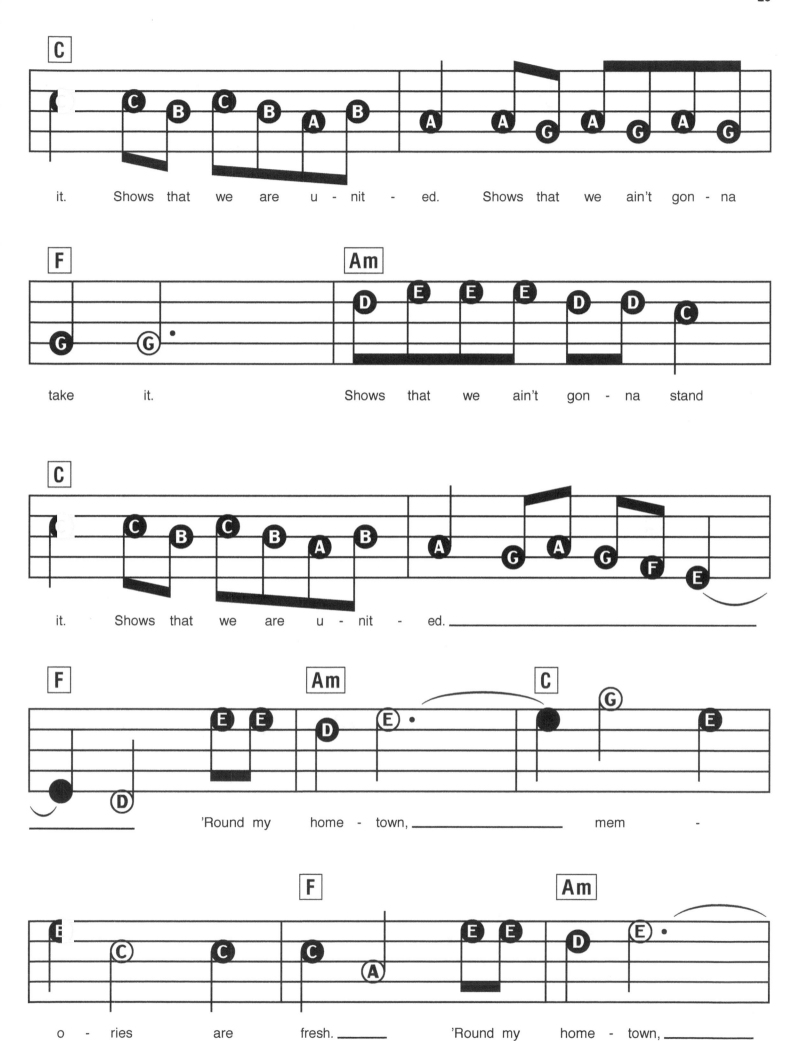

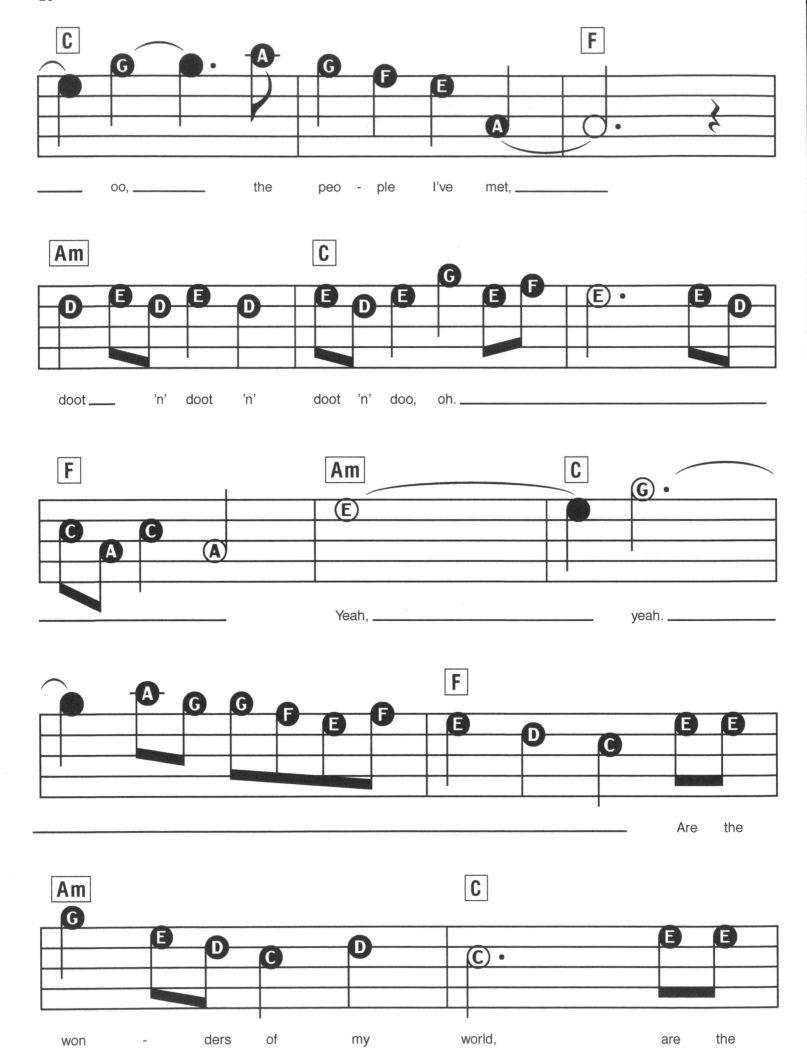

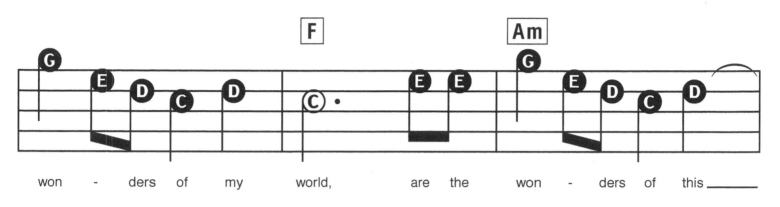

won - ders of my world, are the won - ders of this ____

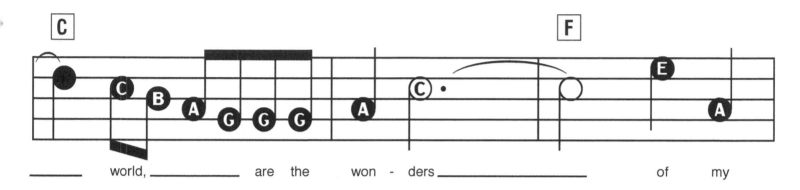

____ world, _____ are the won - ders _____ of my

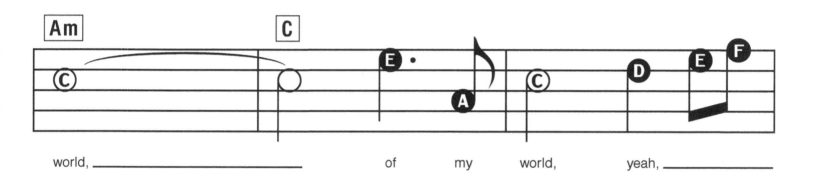

world, _____ of my world, yeah, _____

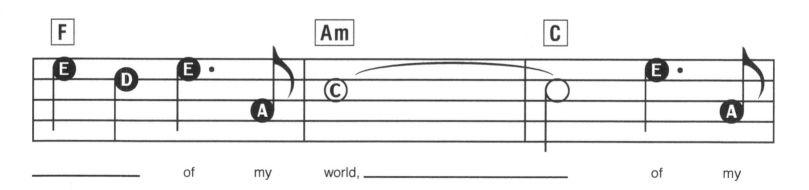

_____ of my world, _____ of my

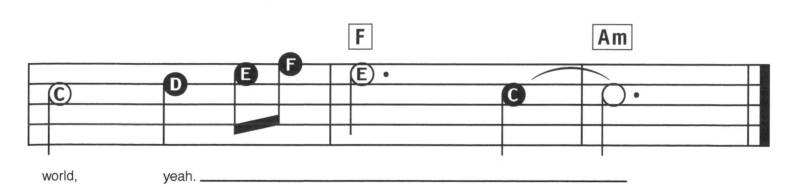

world, yeah. _____

Million Years Ago

Registration 4
Rhythm: Ballad

Words and Music by Adele Adkins
and Gregory Kurstin

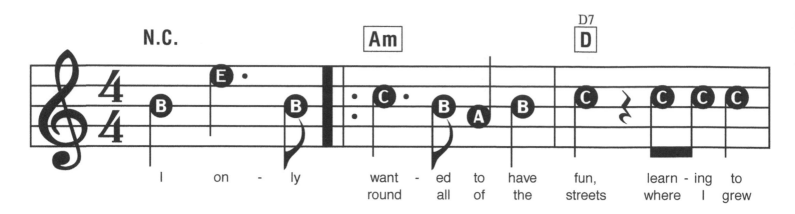

I on - ly want - ed to have fun, learn - ing to
round all of the streets where I grew

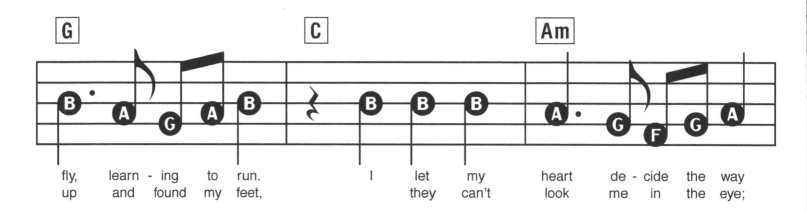

fly, learn - ing to run. I let my heart de - cide the way
up and found my feet, they can't look me in the eye;

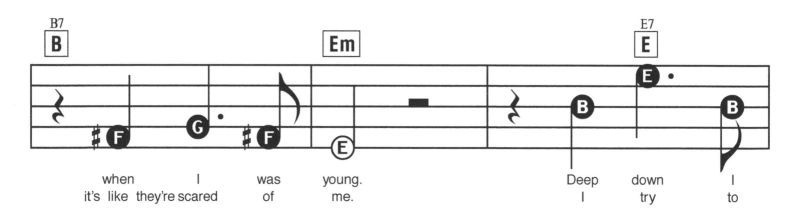

when I was young.
it's like they're scared of me.

Deep down I try to

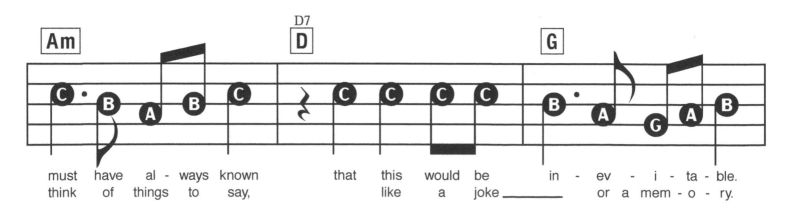

must have al - ways known that this would be in - ev - i - ta - ble.
think of things to say, like a joke _____ or a mem - o - ry.

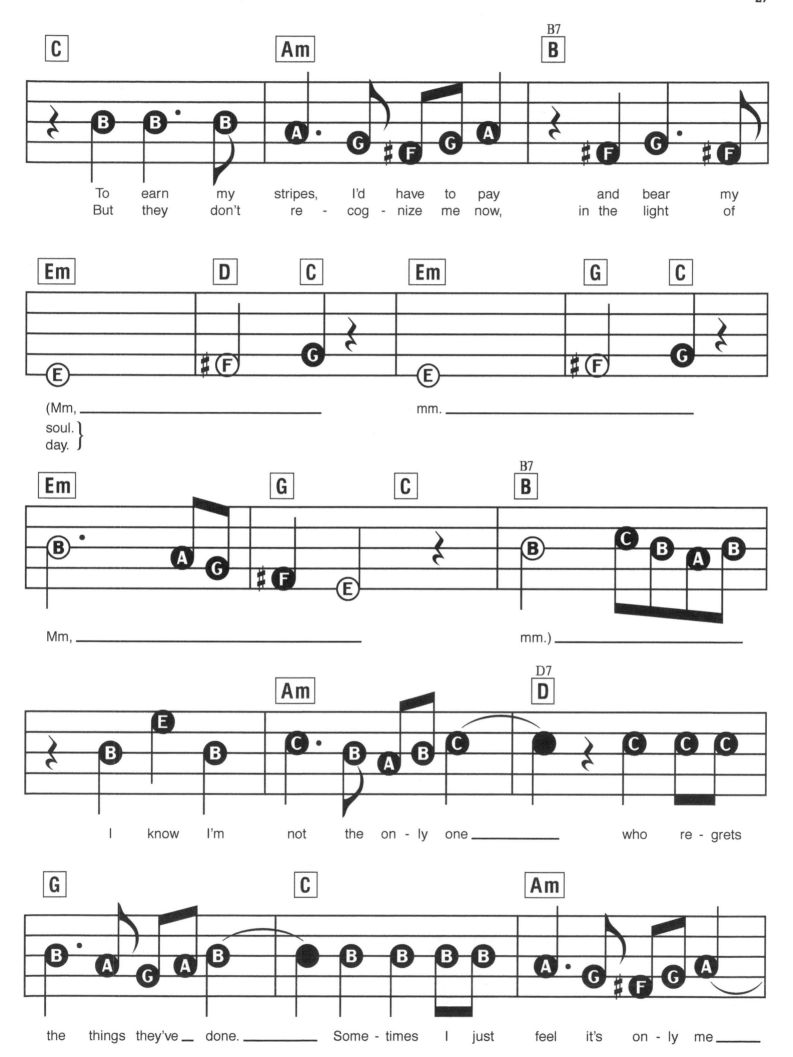

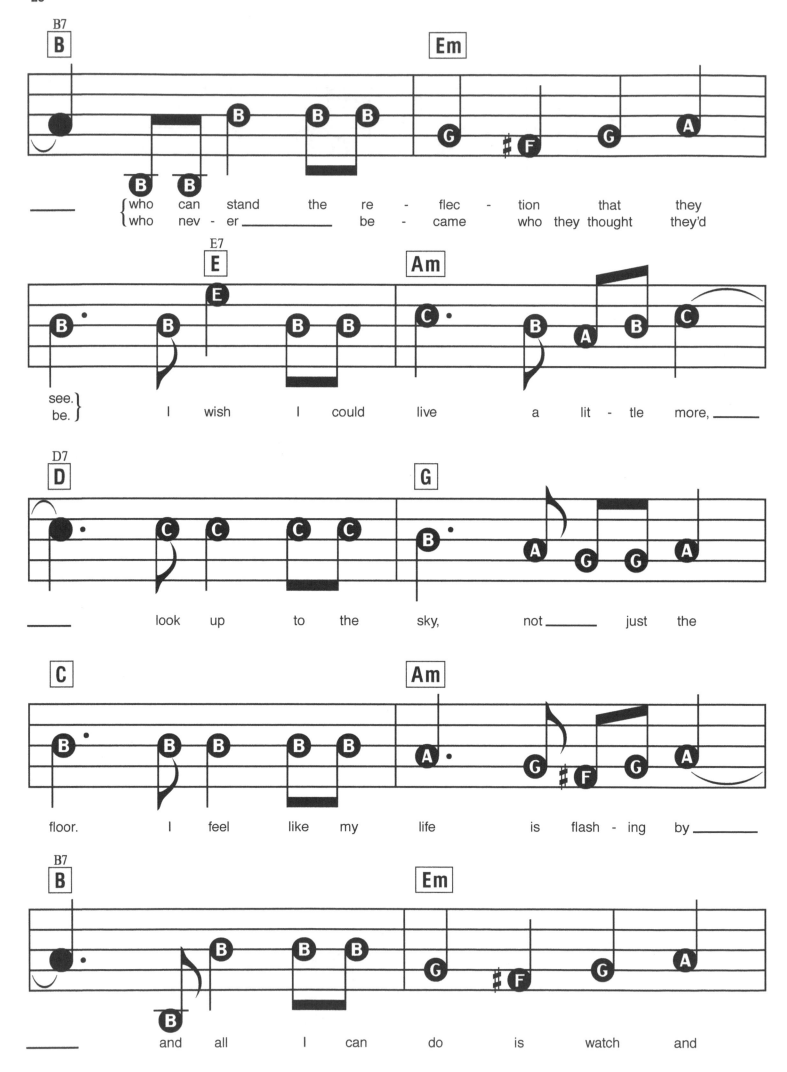

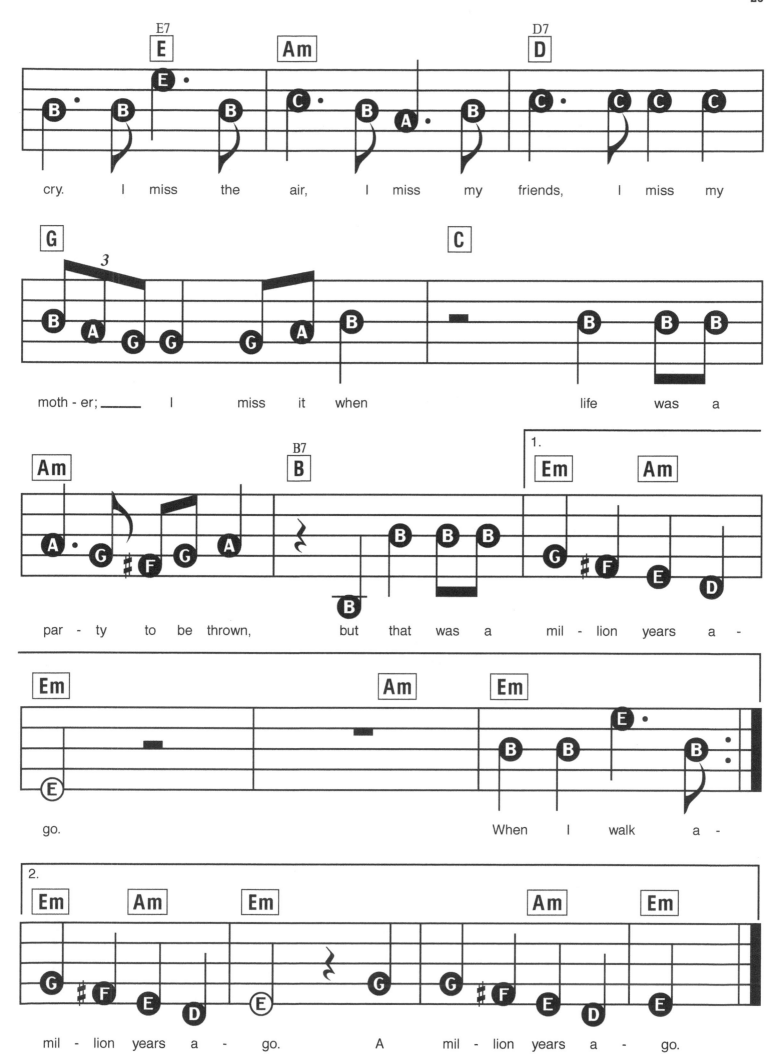

Remedy

Registration 8
Rhythm: 6/8 Ballad

Words and Music by Adele Adkins
and Ryan Tedder

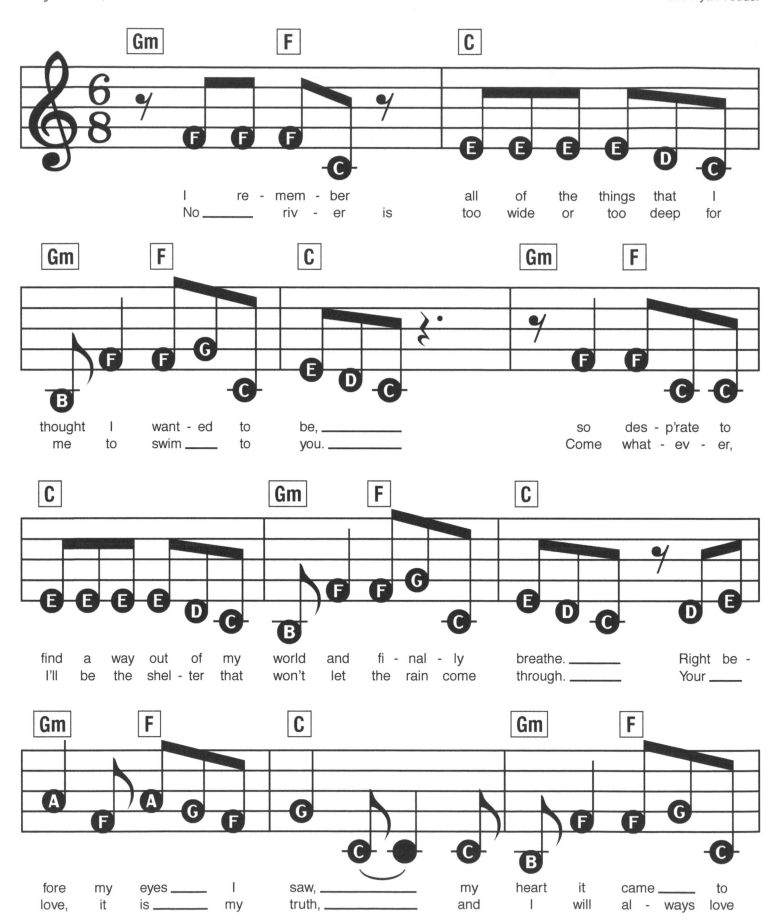

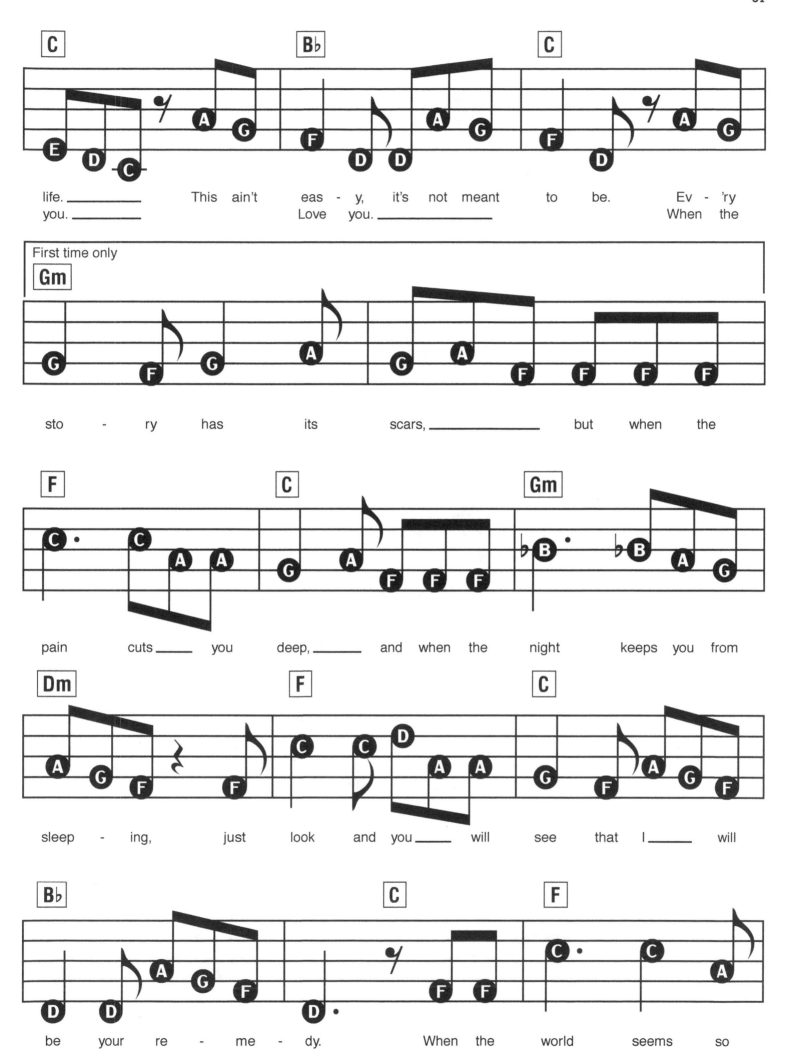

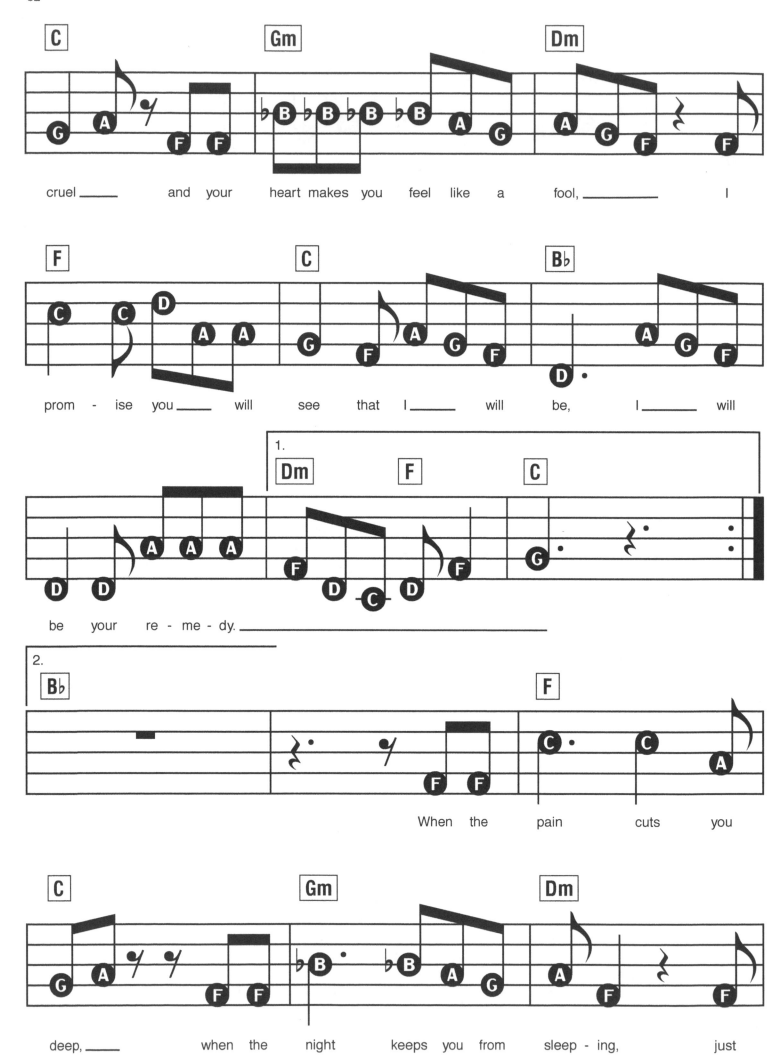

cruel _____ and your heart makes you feel like a fool, _____ I

prom - ise you _____ will see that I _____ will be, I _____ will

1.

be your re - me - dy. _____

2.

When the pain cuts you

deep, _____ when the night keeps you from sleep - ing, just

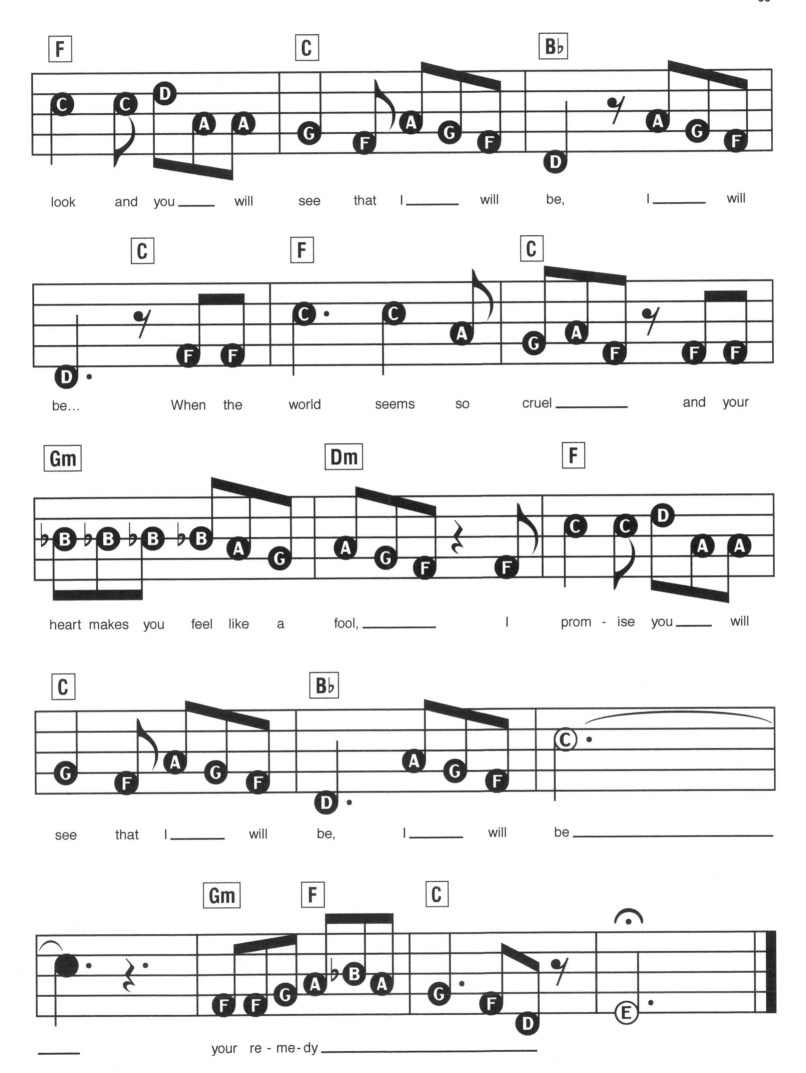

33

Rolling in the Deep

Registration 4
Rhythm: Rock or Pop

Words and Music by Adele Adkins
and Paul Epworth

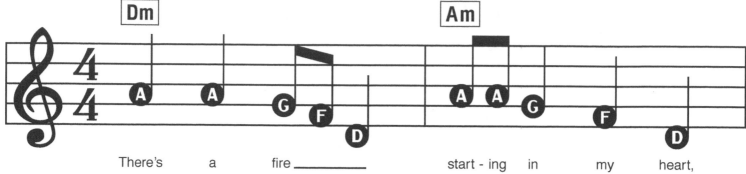

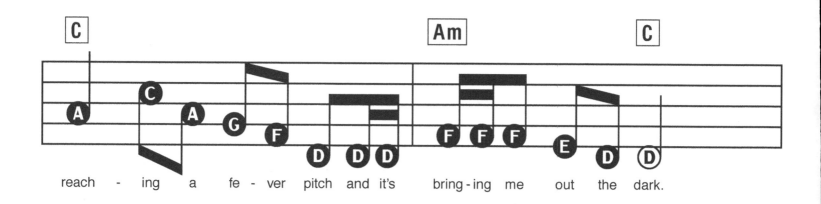

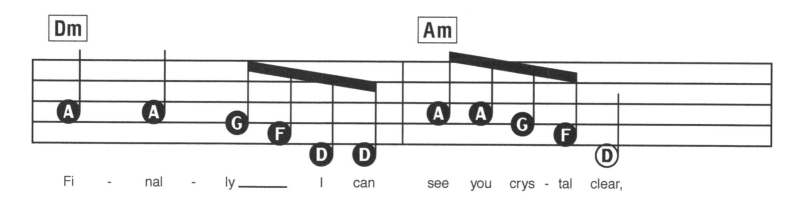

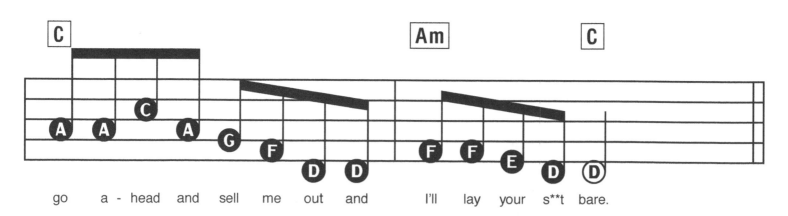

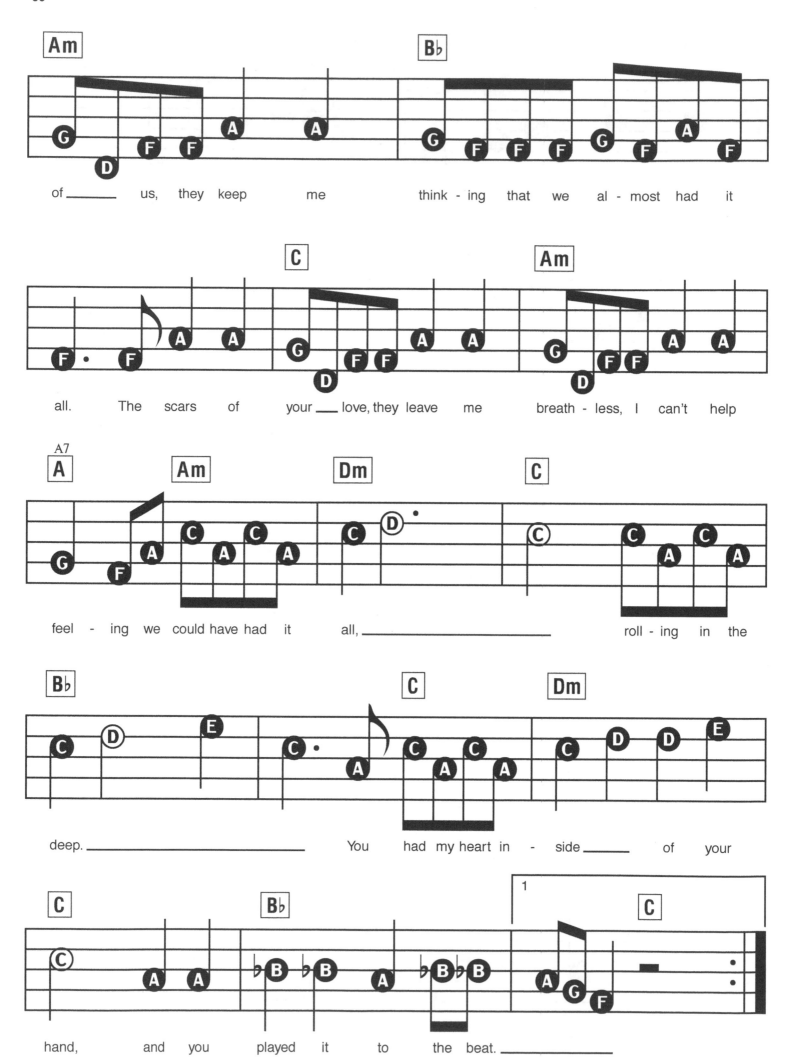

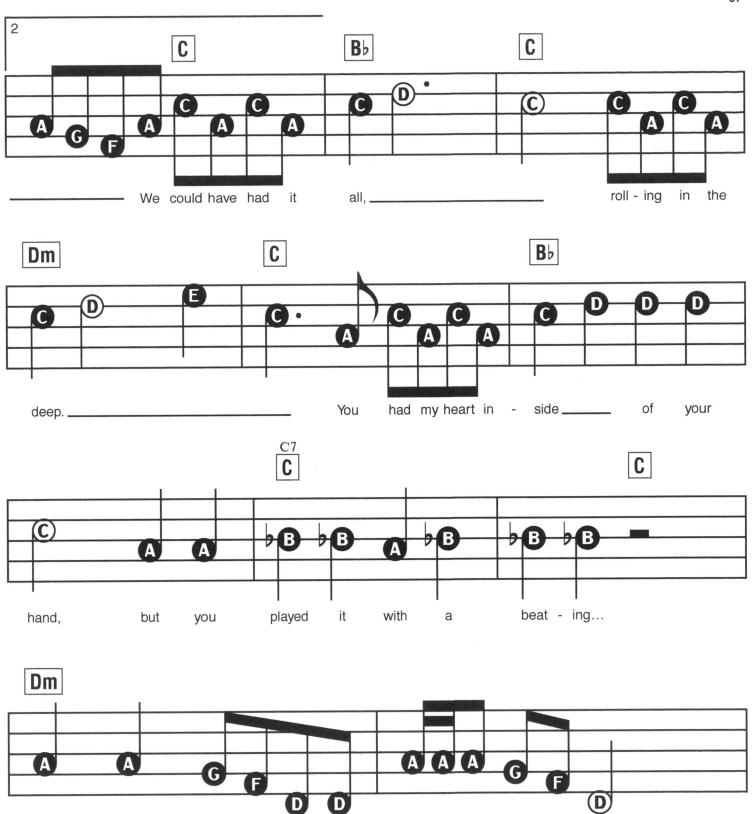

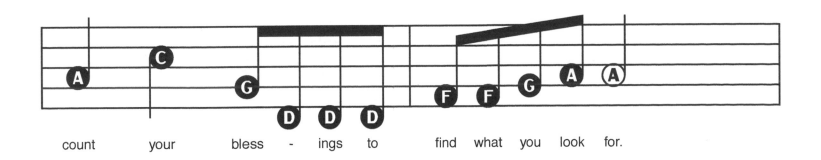

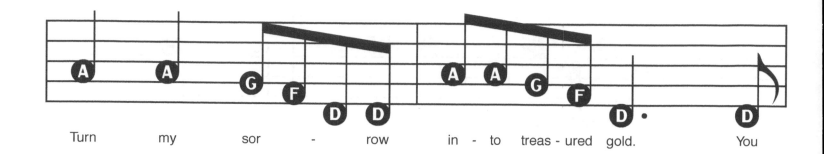

Turn my sor - row in - to treas - ured gold. You

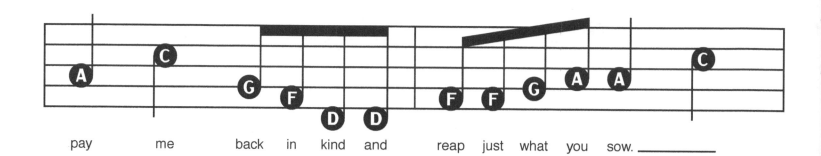

pay me back in kind and reap just what you sow. _____

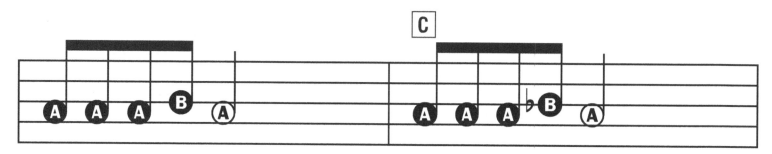

You're gon - na wish you nev - er had met me,

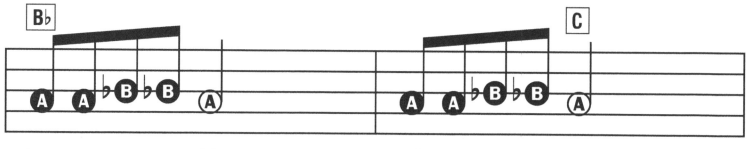

tears are gon - na fall, roll - ing in the deep.

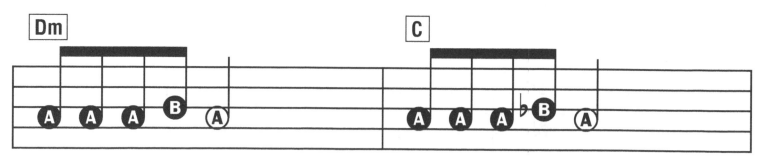

You're gon - na wish you nev - er had met me,

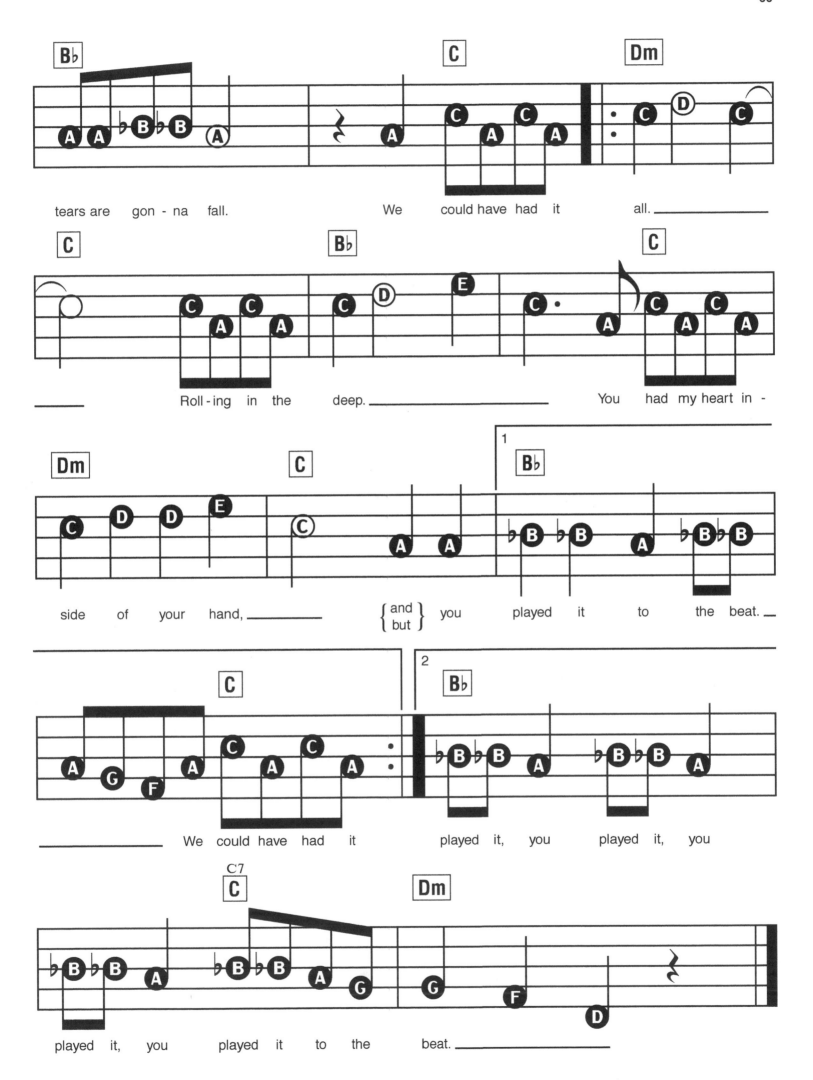

Set Fire to the Rain

Registration 4
Rhythm: 8-Beat or Rock

Words and Music by Adele Adkins
and Fraser Smith

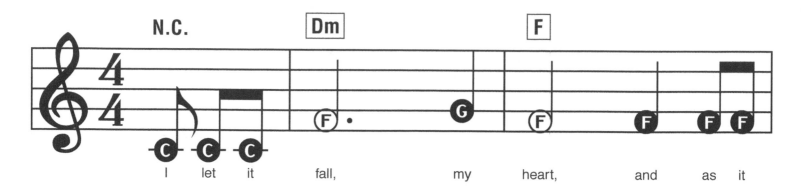

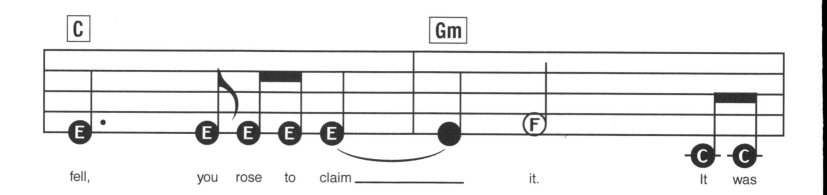

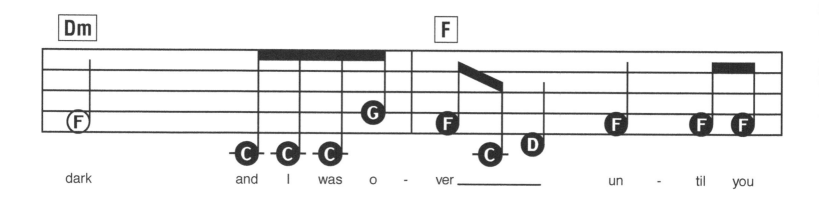

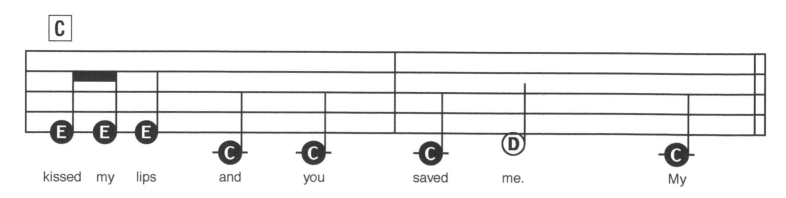

41

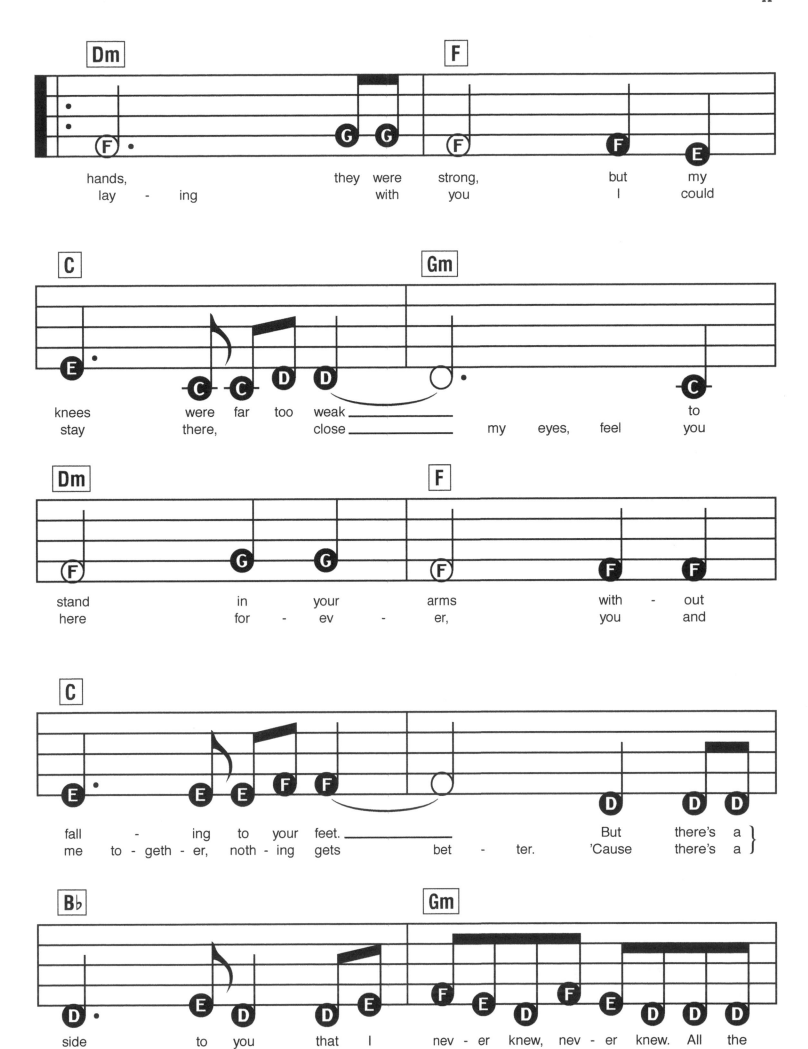

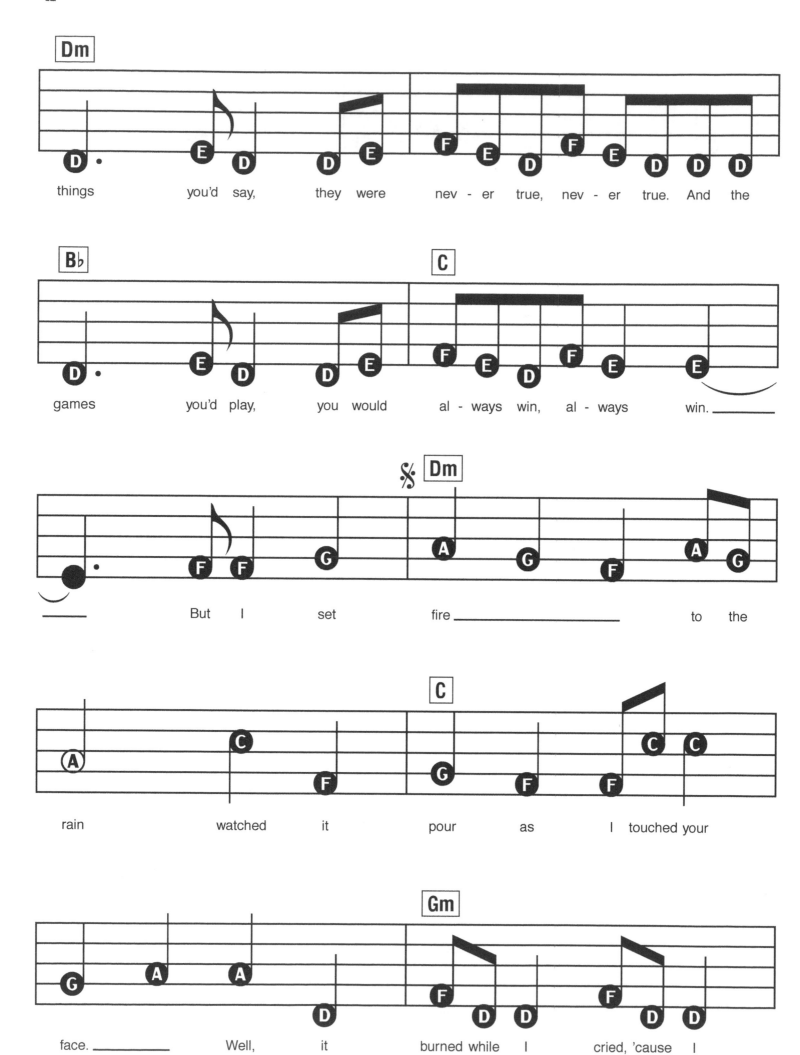

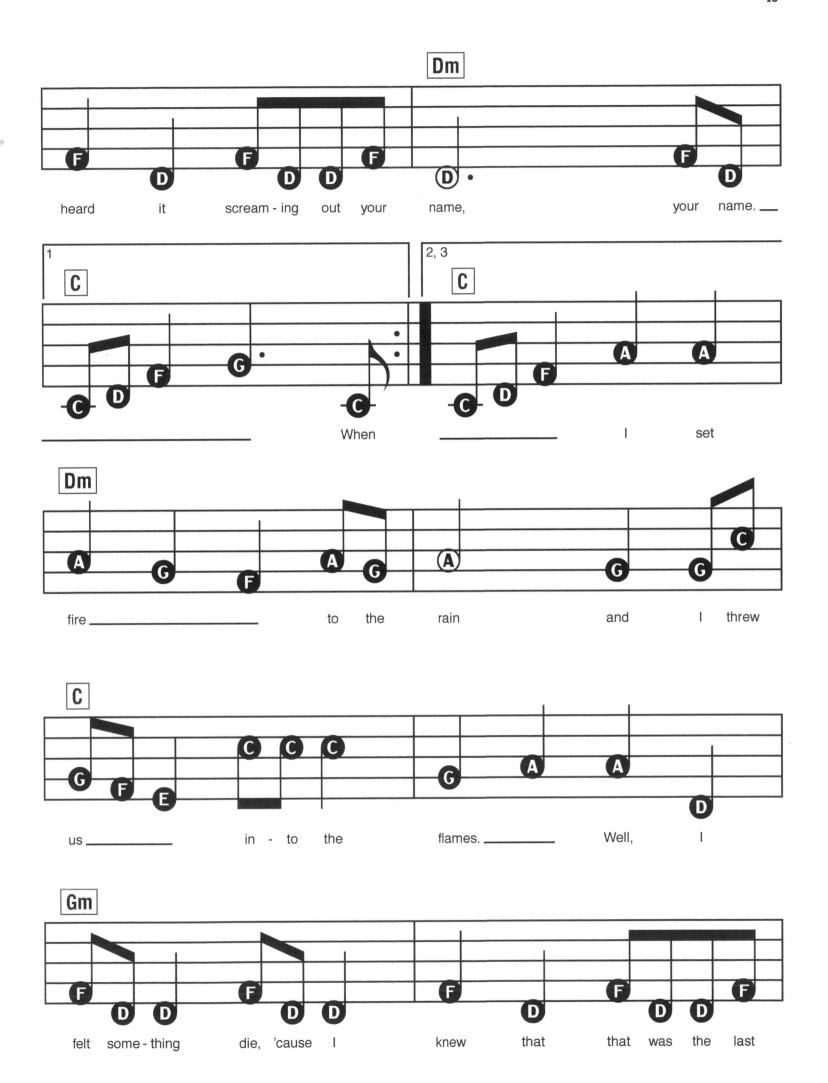

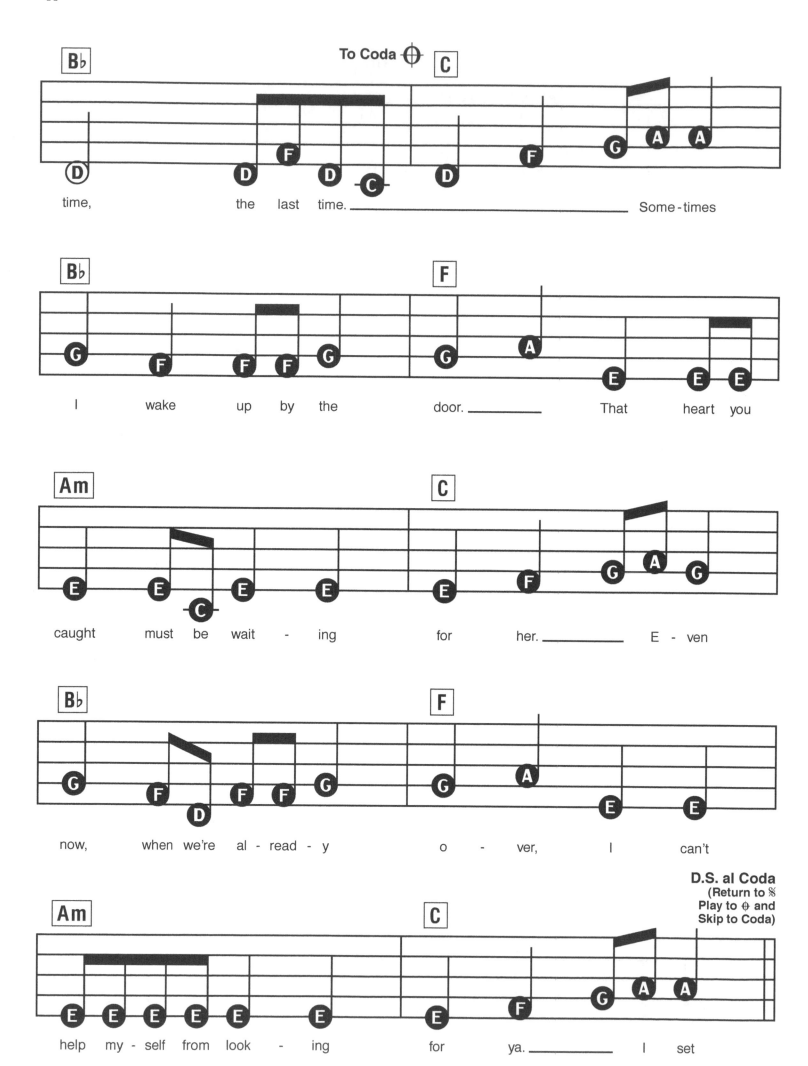

CODA

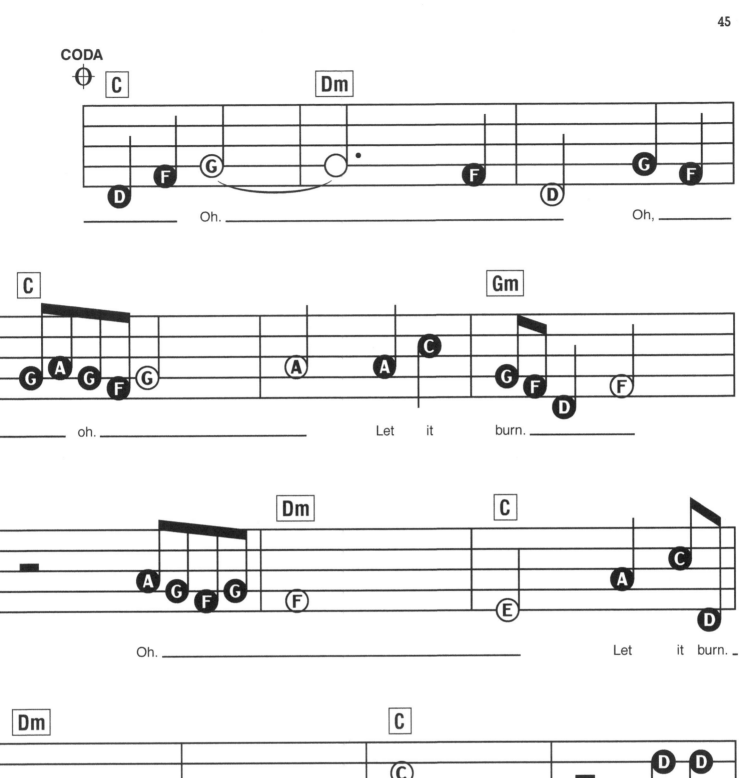

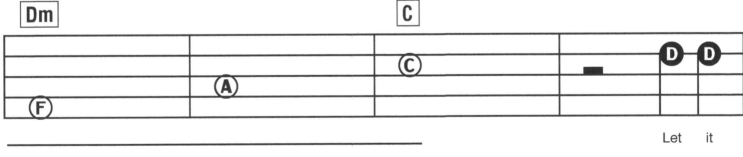

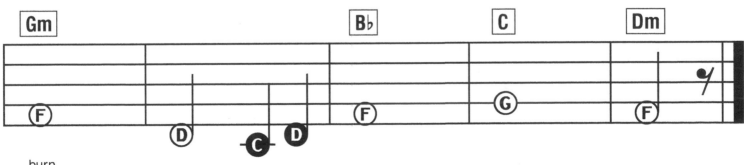

Skyfall

from the Motion Picture SKYFALL

Registration 8
Rhythm: 8-Beat or Ballad

Words and Music by Adele Adkins
and Paul Epworth

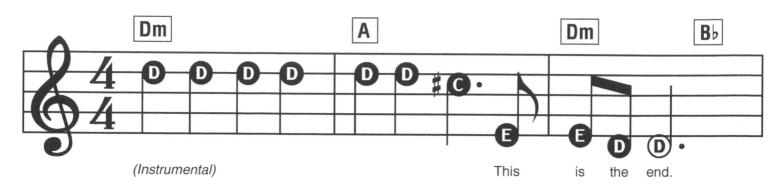

(Instrumental)   This   is   the   end.

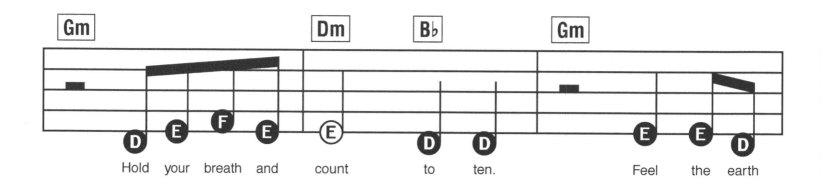

Hold your breath and   count   to   ten.   Feel   the   earth

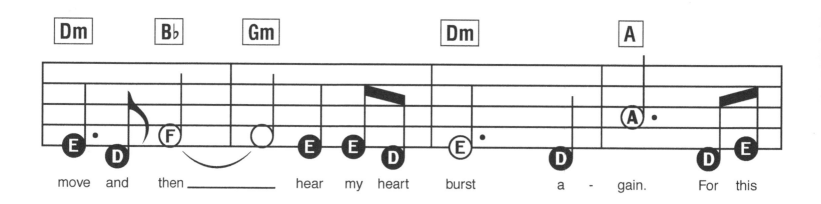

move and then _____ hear my heart burst   a - gain.   For this

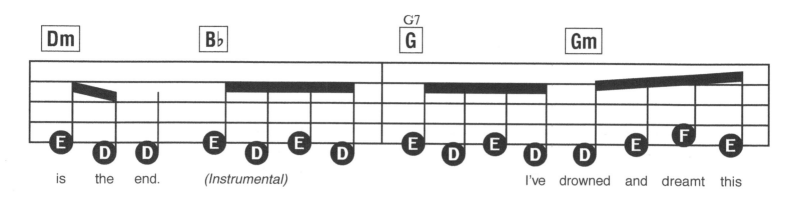

is   the   end.   (Instrumental)   I've drowned and dreamt this

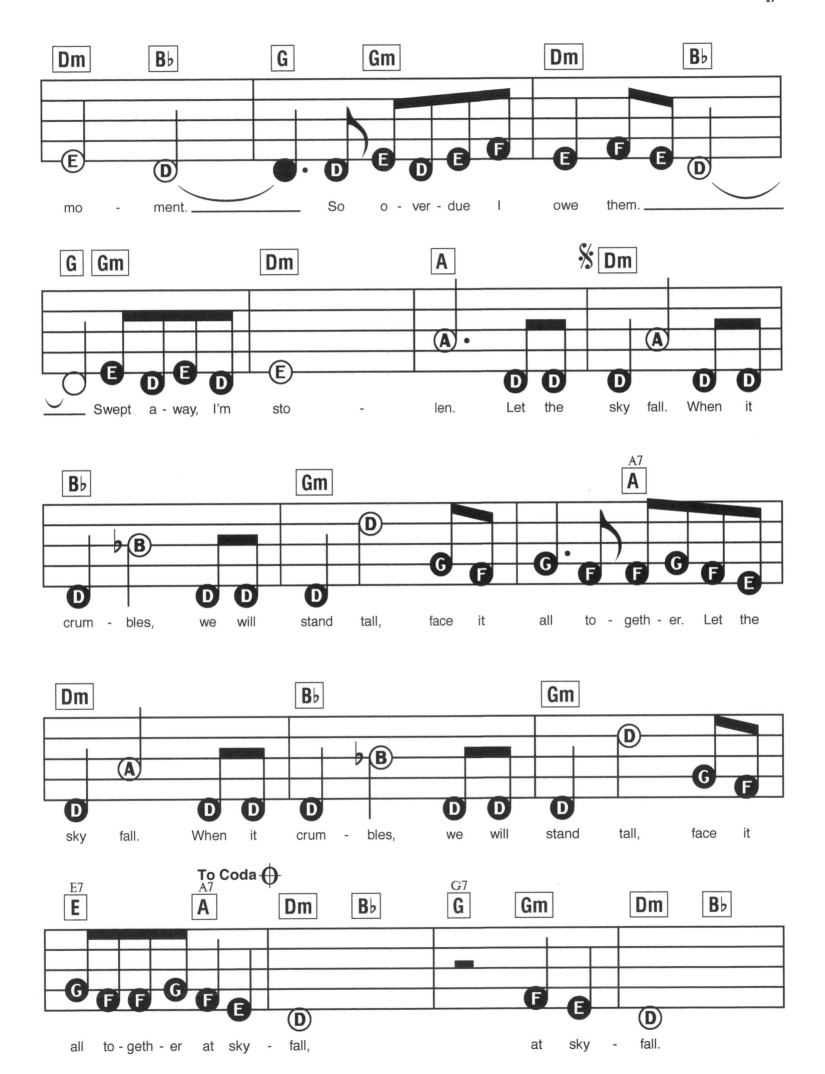

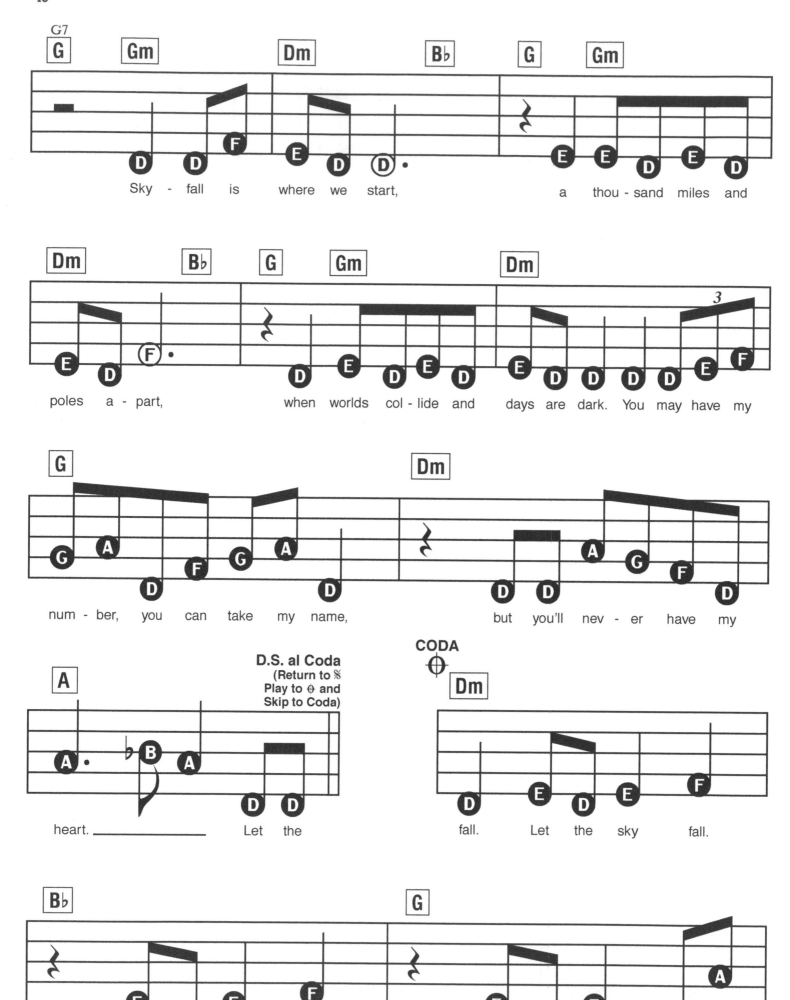

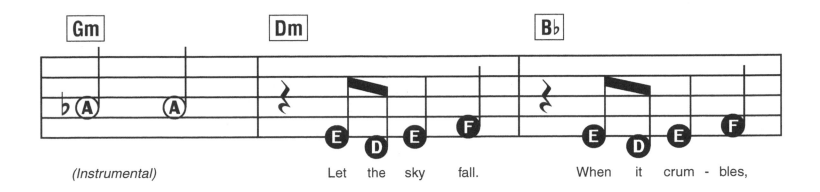

(Instrumental)

Let the sky fall. When it crum - bles,

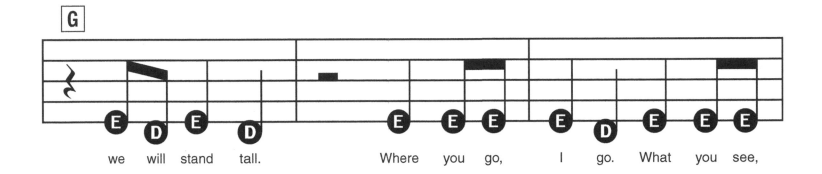

we will stand tall. Where you go, I go. What you see,

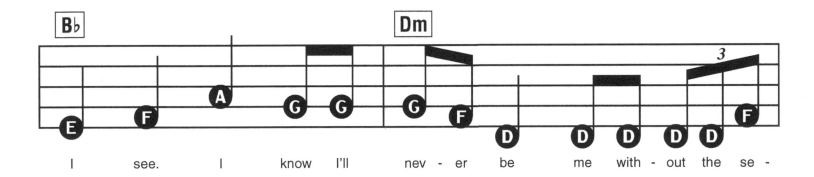

I see. I know I'll nev - er be me with - out the se -

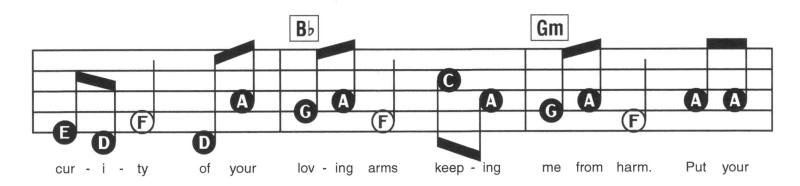

cur - i - ty of your lov - ing arms keep - ing me from harm. Put your

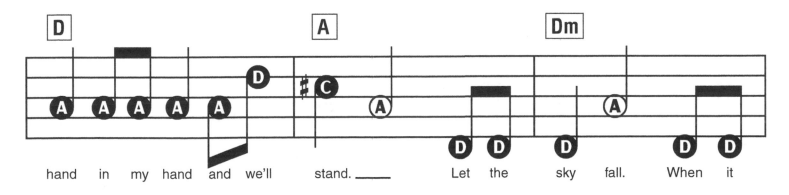

hand in my hand and we'll stand. _____ Let the sky fall. When it

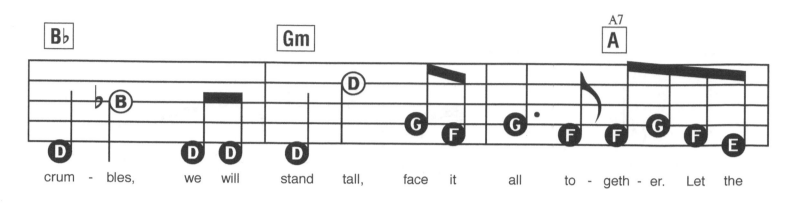

crum - bles, we will stand tall, face it all to - geth - er. Let the

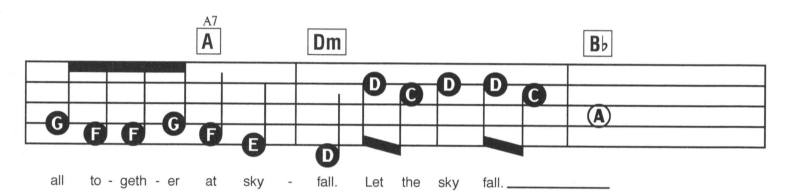

sky fall. When it crum - bles, we will stand tall, face it

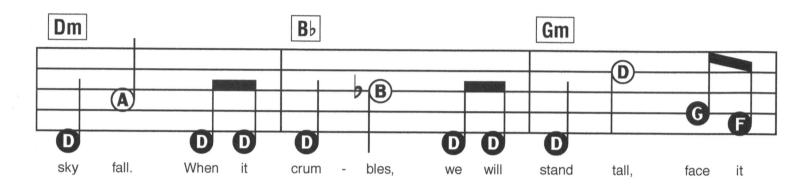

all to - geth - er at sky - fall. Let the sky fall._____

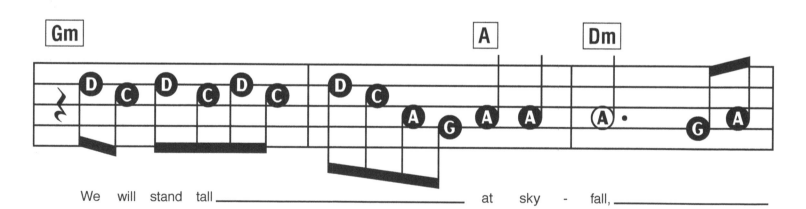

We will stand tall _____ at sky - fall, _____

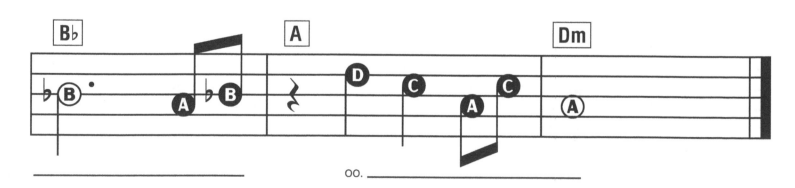

_____ oo. _____

Someone Like You

Registration 2
Rhythm: 4/4 Ballad

Words and Music by Adele Adkins
and Dan Wilson

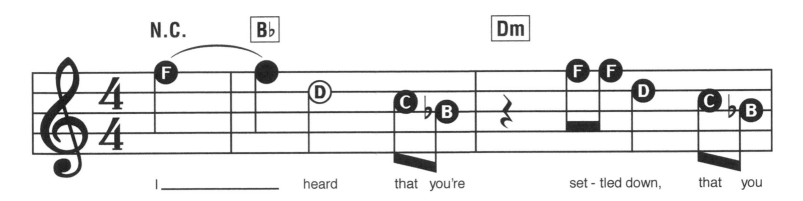

I _____ heard that you're set - tled down, that you

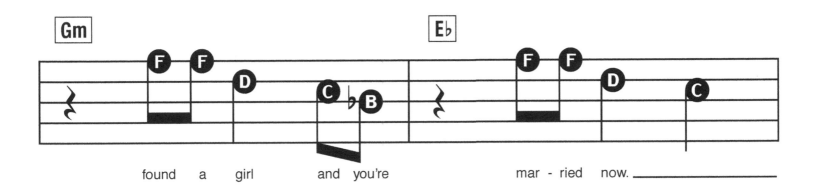

found a girl and you're mar - ried now. _____

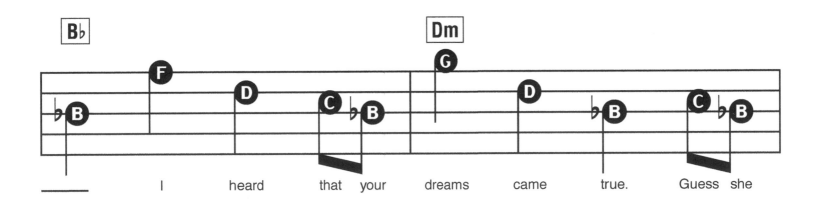

_____ I heard that your dreams came true. Guess she

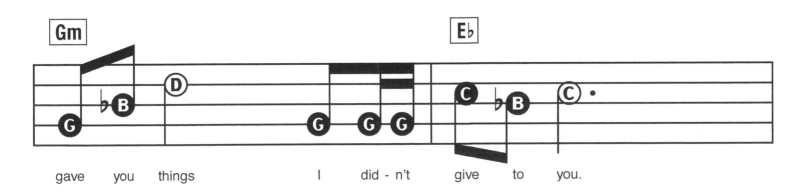

gave you things I did - n't give to you.

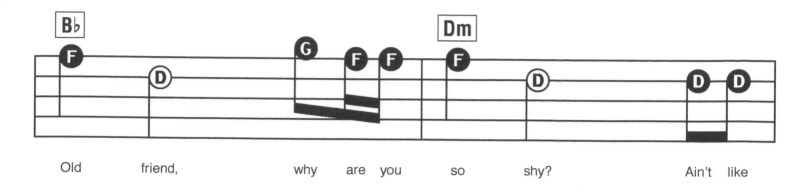

Old friend, why are you so shy? Ain't like

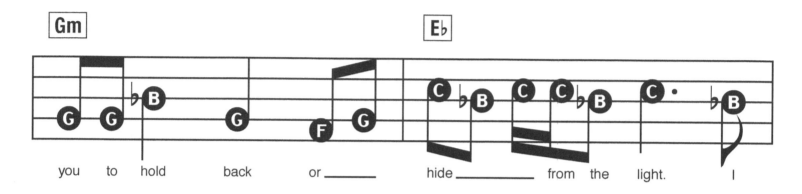

you to hold back or _____ hide _____ from the light. I

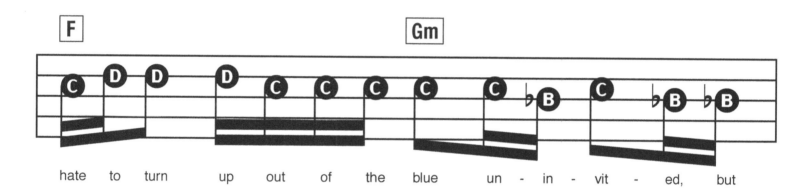

hate to turn up out of the blue un - in - vit - ed, but

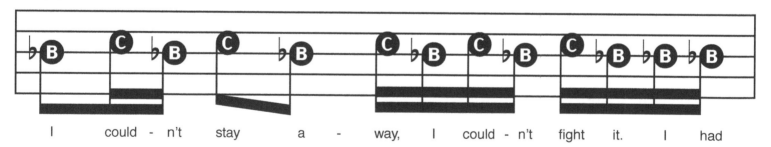

I could - n't stay a - way, I could - n't fight it. I had

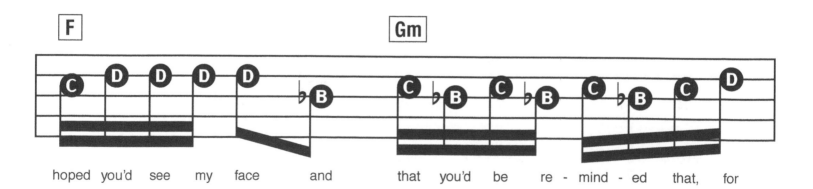

hoped you'd see my face and that you'd be re - mind - ed that, for

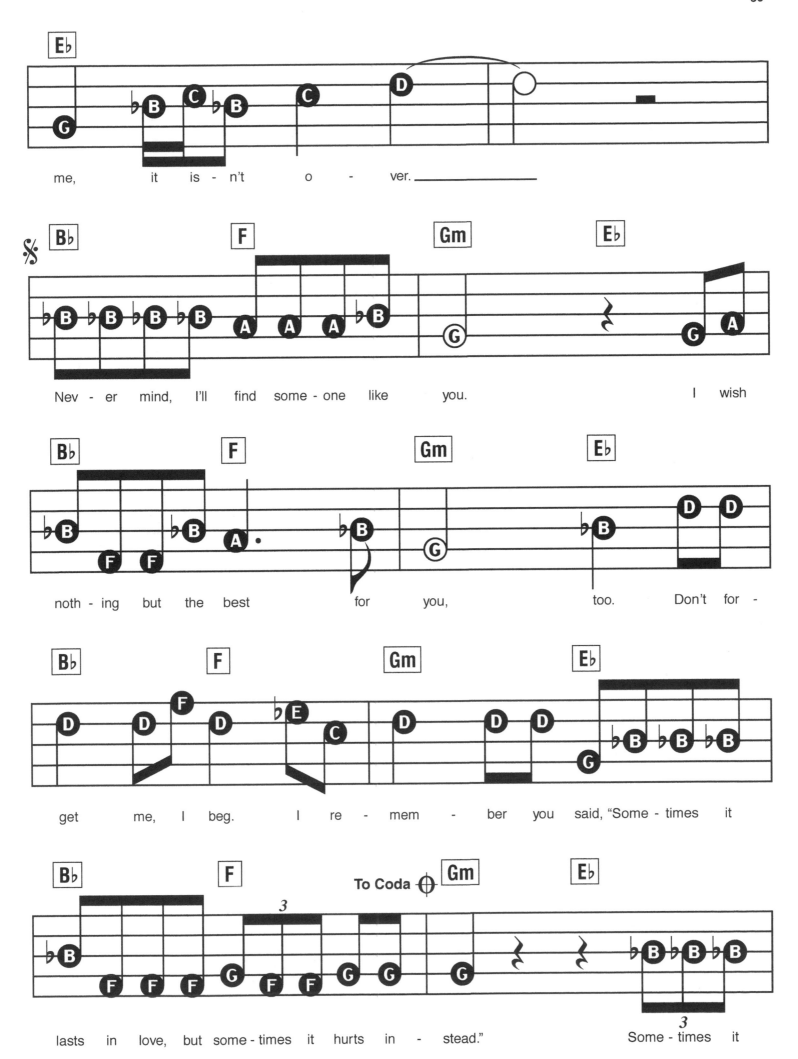

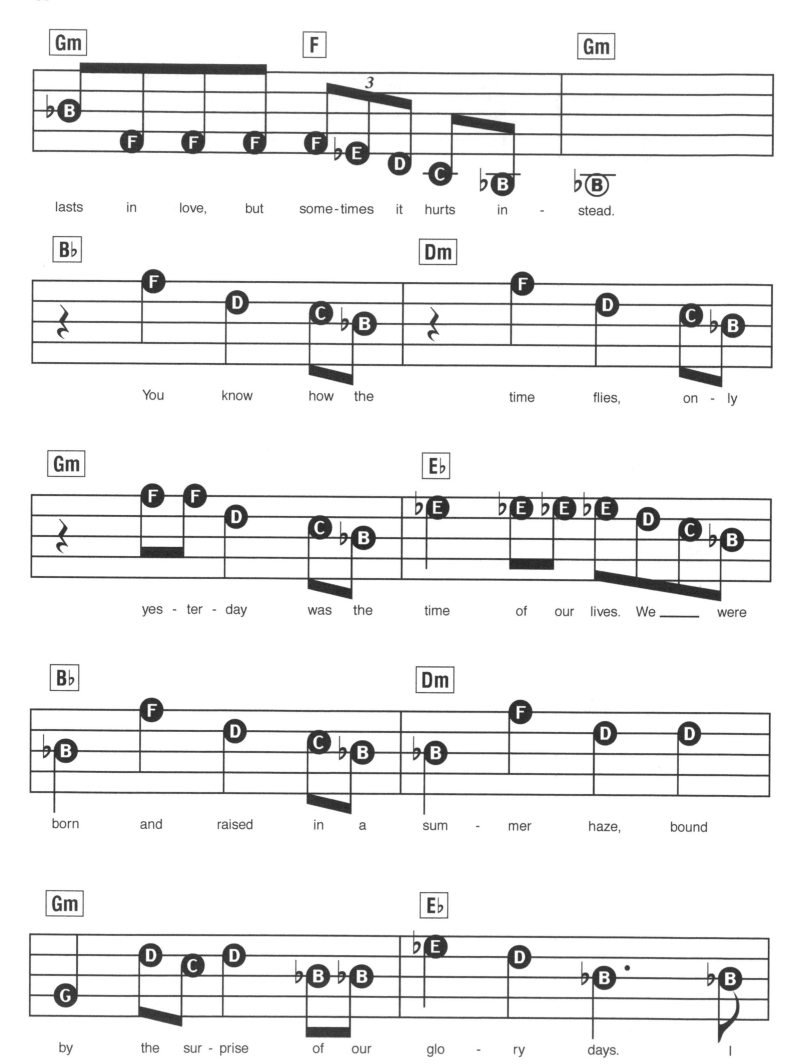

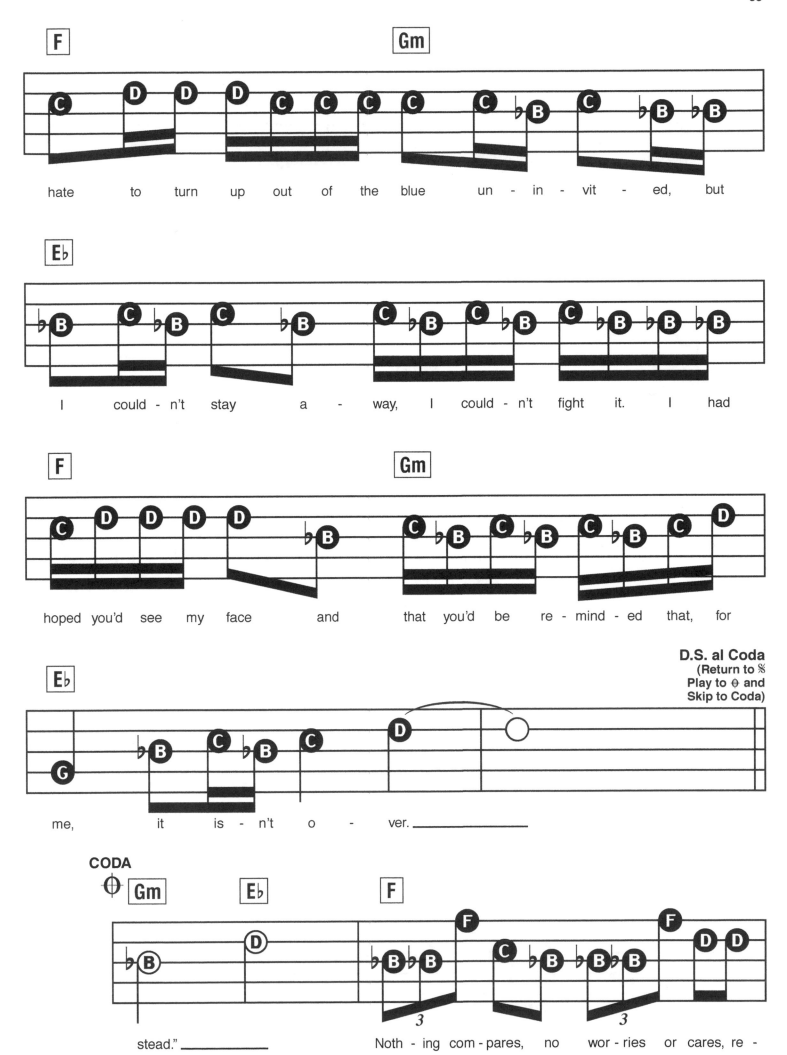

F

Gm

hate to turn up out of the blue un - in - vit - ed, but

Eb

I could - n't stay a - way, I could - n't fight it. I had

F

Gm

hoped you'd see my face and that you'd be re - mind - ed that, for

D.S. al Coda
(Return to %
Play to ⊕ and
Skip to Coda)

Eb

me, it is - n't o - ver. _____

CODA
⊕ Gm

Eb

F

stead." _____

Noth - ing com - pares, no wor - ries or cares, re -

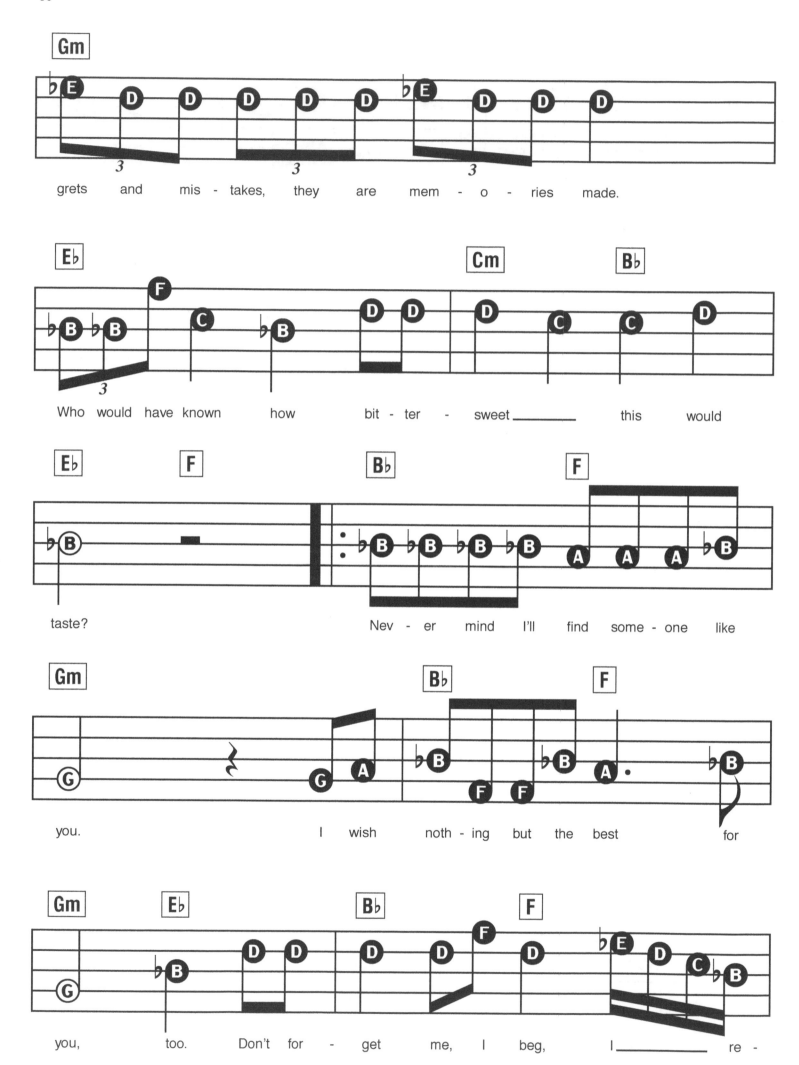

Gm

grets and mis - takes, they are mem - o - ries made.

Eb   **Cm**   **Bb**

Who would have known how bit - ter - sweet _____ this would

Eb   **F**   **Bb**   **F**

taste? Nev - er mind I'll find some - one like

Gm   **Bb**   **F**

you. I wish noth - ing but the best for

Gm   **Eb**   **Bb**   **F**

you, too. Don't for - get me, I beg, I _____ re -

57

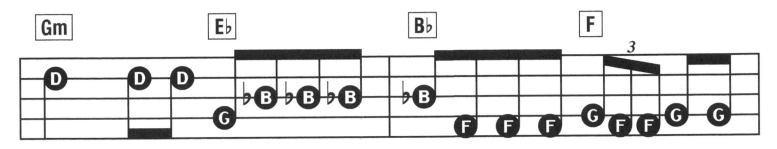

mem - ber you said, "Some - times it lasts in love, but some - times it hurts in -

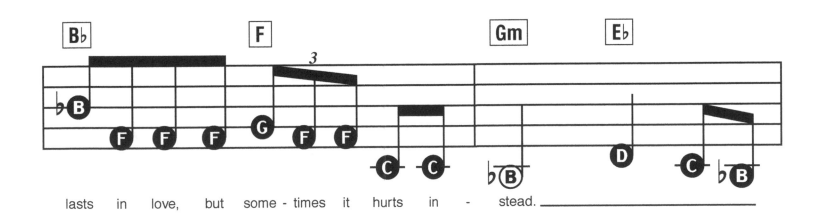

stead." _____   stead." _____ Some - times it

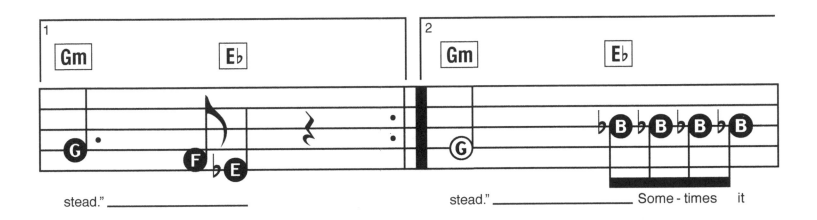

lasts in love, but some - times it hurts in - stead. _____

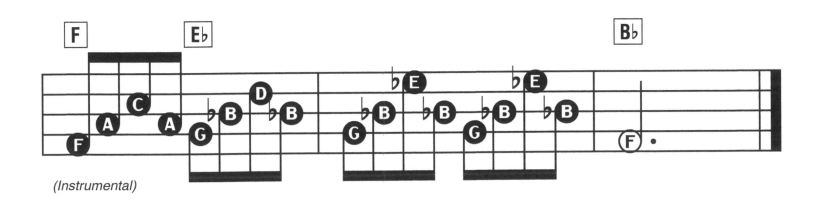

(Instrumental)

When We Were Young

Registration 8
Rhythm: Ballad

Words and Music by Adele Adkins
and Tobias Jesso Jr.

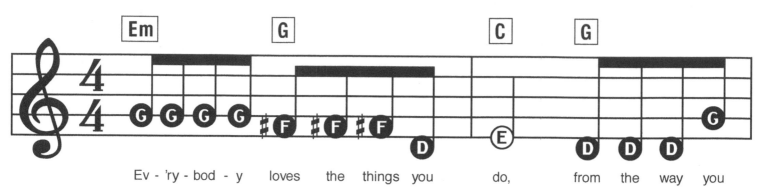

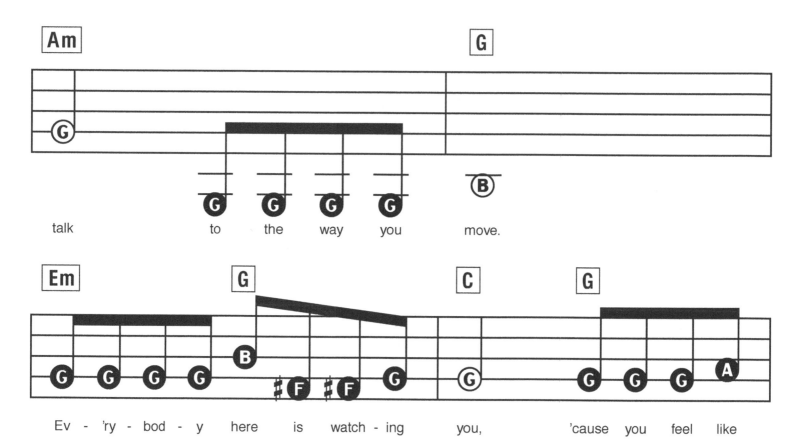

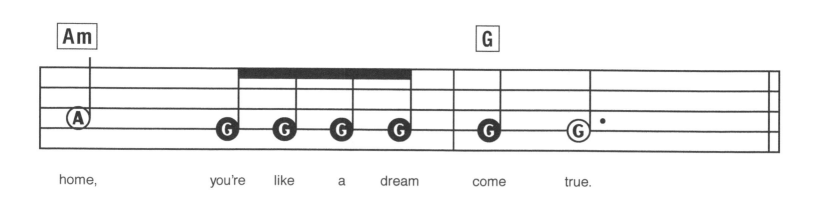

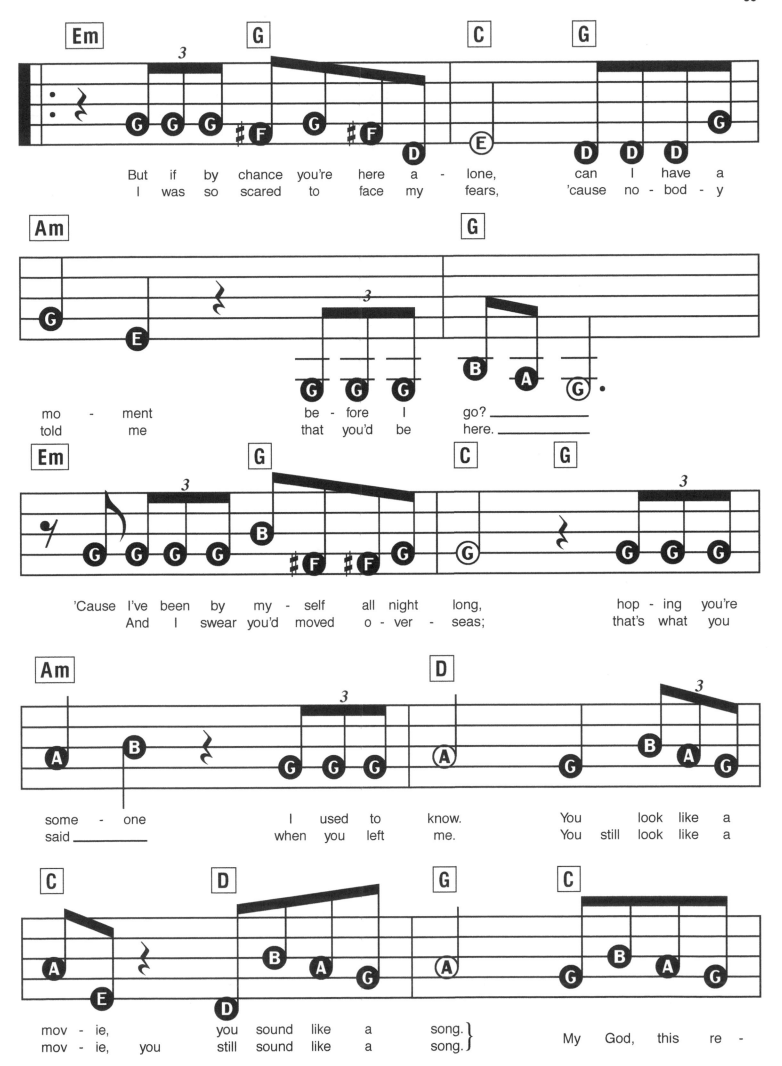

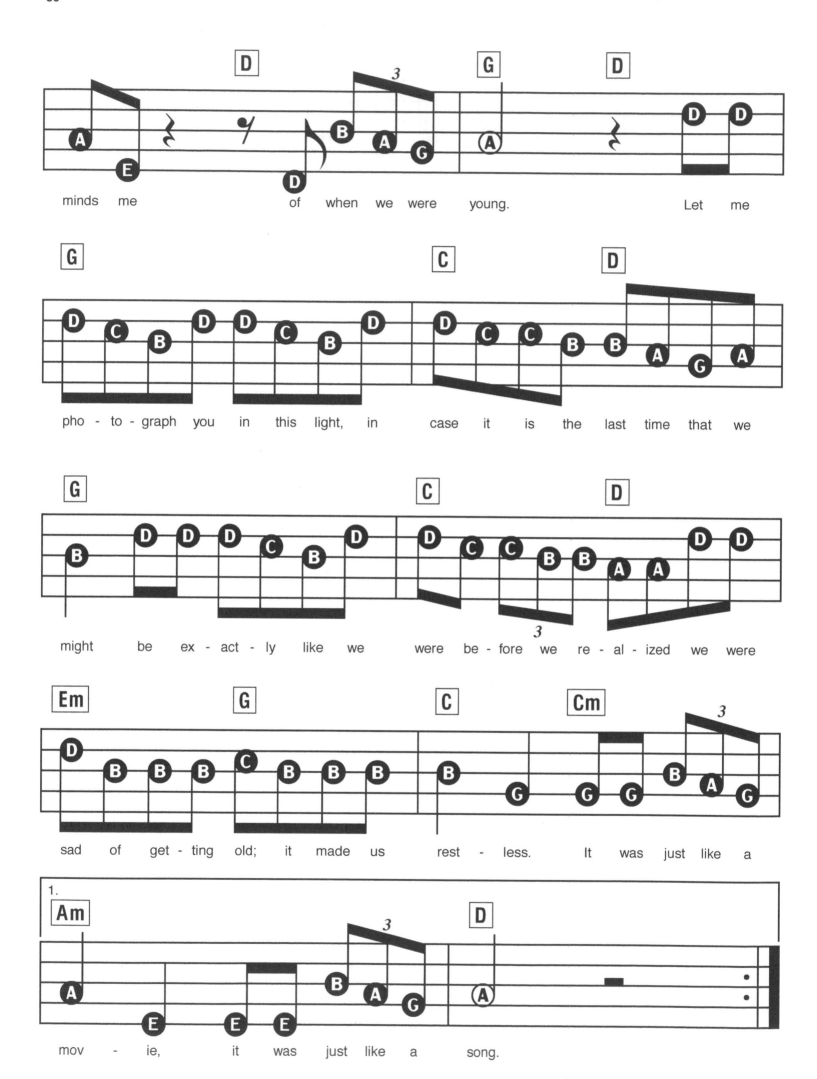

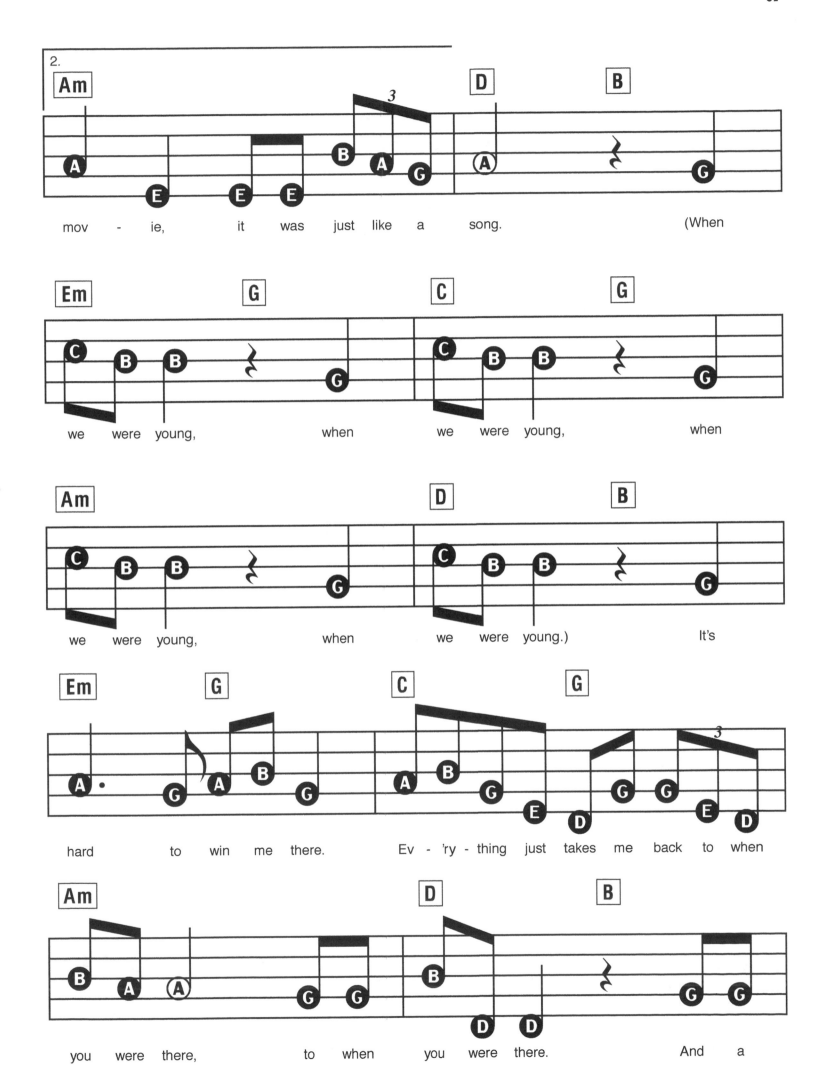

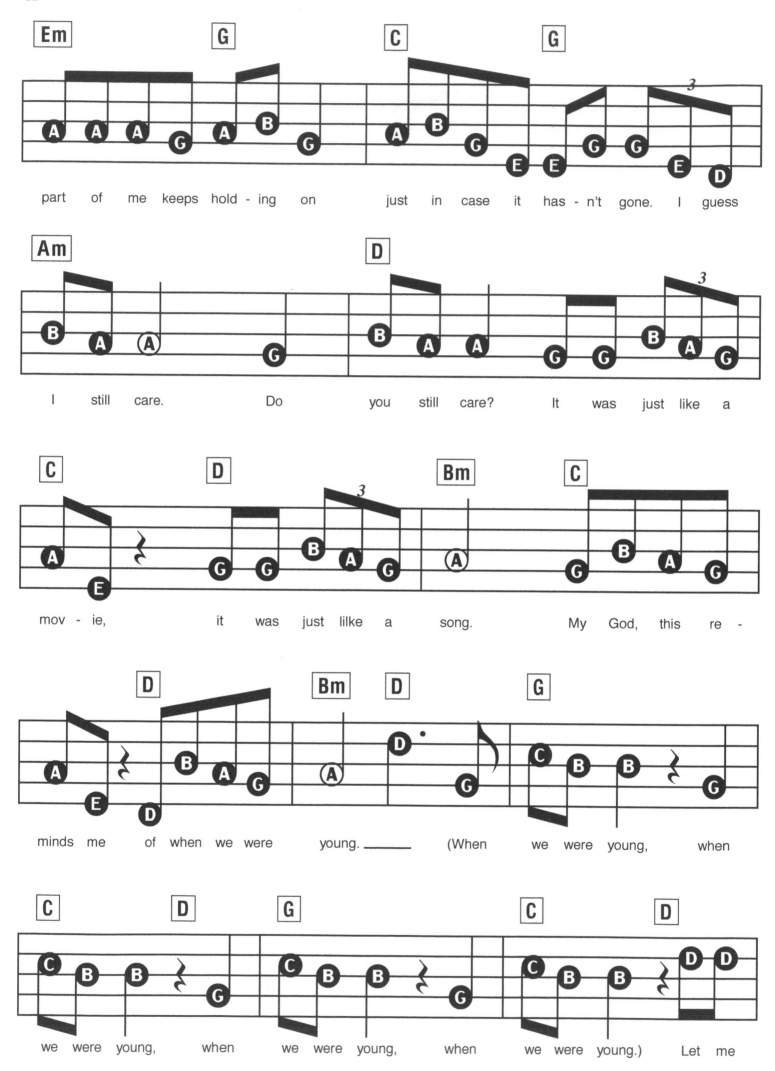

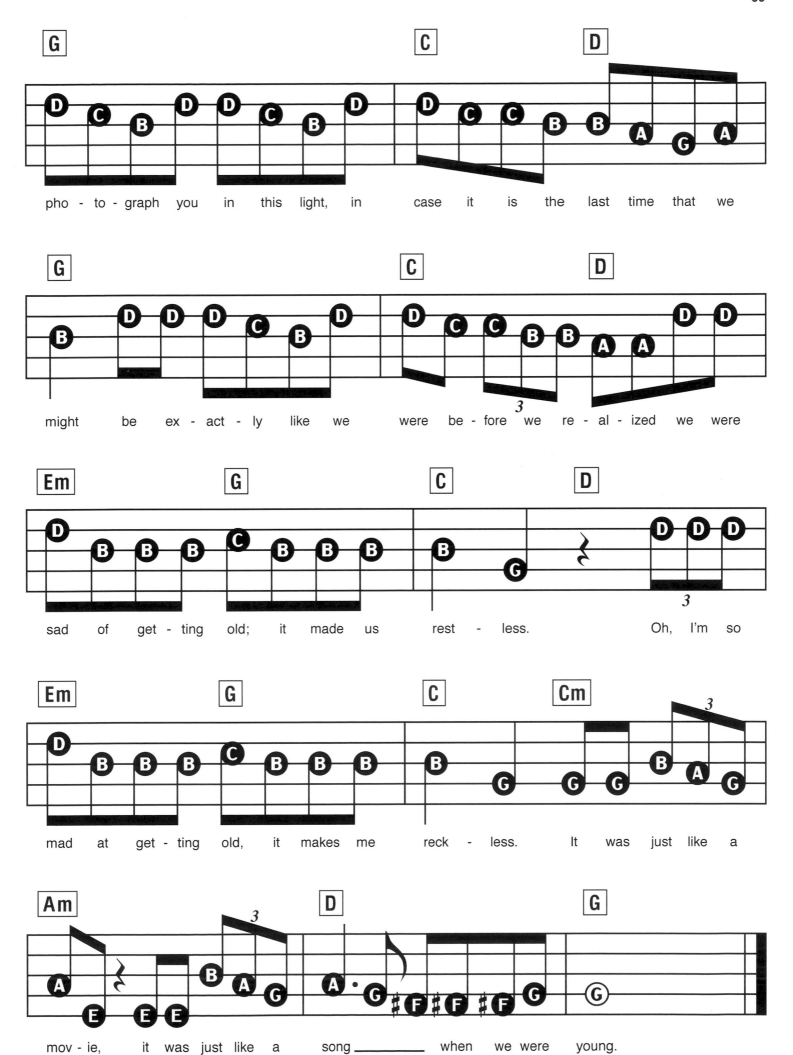

Registration Guide

- Match the Registration number on the song to the corresponding numbered category below. Select and activate an instrumental sound available on your instrument.

- Choose an automatic rhythm appropriate to the mood and style of the song. (Consult your Owner's Guide for proper operation of automatic rhythm features.)

- Adjust the tempo and volume controls to comfortable settings.

Registration

1	Mellow	Flutes, Clarinet, Oboe, Flugel Horn, Trombone, French Horn, Organ Flutes
2	Ensemble	Brass Section, Sax Section, Wind Ensemble, Full Organ, Theater Organ
3	Strings	Violin, Viola, Cello, Fiddle, String Ensemble, Pizzicato, Organ Strings
4	Guitars	Acoustic/Electric Guitars, Banjo, Mandolin, Dulcimer, Ukulele, Hawaiian Guitar
5	Mallets	Vibraphone, Marimba, Xylophone, Steel Drums, Bells, Celesta, Chimes
6	Liturgical	Pipe Organ, Hand Bells, Vocal Ensemble, Choir, Organ Flutes
7	Bright	Saxophones, Trumpet, Mute Trumpet, Synth Leads, Jazz/Gospel Organs
8	Piano	Piano, Electric Piano, Honky Tonk Piano, Harpsichord, Clavi
9	Novelty	Melodic Percussion, Wah Trumpet, Synth, Whistle, Kazoo, Perc. Organ
10	Bellows	Accordion, French Accordion, Mussette, Harmonica, Pump Organ, Bagpipes